Royal College of Physicians of Edinburgh

**Historical Sketch and Laws of the Royal College of Physicians, of Edinburgh, from its institution to August, 1882**

Royal College of Physicians of Edinburgh

**Historical Sketch and Laws of the Royal College of Physicians, of Edinburgh, from its institution to August, 1882**

ISBN/EAN: 9783337163136

Printed in Europe, USA, Canada, Australia, Japan

Cover: Foto ©ninafisch / pixelio.de

More available books at **www.hansebooks.com**

# HISTORICAL SKETCH

AND

# LAWS

OF THE

# ROYAL COLLEGE OF PHYSICIANS

OF

# EDINBURGH,

FROM

*ITS INSTITUTION TO AUGUST 1882.*

EDINBURGH:
PRINTED FOR THE ROYAL COLLEGE OF PHYSICIANS.
1882.

# OFFICE BEARERS.
## 1882.

**President.**
DANIEL RUTHERFORD HALDANE.

**Vice-President.**
ALEXANDER PEDDIE.

**Council.**
THE PRESIDENT.

| | |
|---|---|
| THE VICE-PRESIDENT. | ANDREW DOUGLAS MACLAGAN. |
| ALEXANDER KEILLER. | CLAUD MUIRHEAD. |
| GEORGE WILLIAM BALFOUR. | JOHN BATTY TUKE. |

**Treasurer.**
JOHN ALEXANDER SMITH.

**Secretary.**
JOHN WYLLIE.

**Librarian.**
GEORGE WILLIAM BALFOUR.

**Curator of Museum.**
THOMAS ALEXANDER GOLDIE BALFOUR.

**Under Librarian.**
JOHN SMALL, M.A.

**Auditor.**
JOHN TURNBULL SMITH, C.A.

**Clerk.**
CHRISTOPHER DOUGLAS, W.S.

*Officer*—JOHN BROOME.

# CONTENTS.

|  | PAGE |
|---|---|
| LIST OF THE FELLOWS OF THE ROYAL COLLEGE OF PHYSICIANS OF EDINBURGH— | |
|     List of those in the Original Patent, | 1 |
|     List of Fellows admitted, | 1 |
| LIST OF HONORARY MEMBERS, | 14 |
| LIST OF PRESIDENTS, | 15 |
| HISTORICAL SKETCH, | 19 |
| LAWS— | |
|     Chapter I. Of the College and Common Seal, | 97 |
|     Chapter II. Of Fellows, | 98 |
|     Chapter III. Of Members, | 101 |
|     Chapter IV. Of Licentiates, | 104 |
|     Chapter V. Of the Fees, | 105 |
|     Chapter VI. Of Forfeiture of Fellowships, Memberships, and Licences, | 106 |
|     Chapter VII. On the Election of Office-Bearers, | 108 |
|     Chapter VIII. Of the Powers and Duties of the Office-Bearers, | 110 |
|     Chapter IX. Of the Meetings of the College, | 120 |
|     Chapter X. Of the Order of Business, | 121 |
|     Chapter XI. Motions, Laws, and Protests, | 123 |
|     Chapter XII. Of the Contributions and Fines, | 126 |
|     Chapter XIII. Of the Property of the College, | 128 |
|     Chapter XIV. Library and Library Committee | 130 |
|     Chapter XV. Museum and Museum Committee, | 134 |
|     Chapter XVI. Of Diplomas, etc., | 135 |
|     Chapter XVII. Certificates of Qualification to Lecture, | 136 |
| APPENDIX, | 139 |
|     Charta Erectionis, | 145 |
|     Charter of Ratification, | 155 |
|     Royal Warrant for Charter of Incorporation, | 160 |
|     Charta Incorporationis, | 171 |

# List

OF

# The Fellows of the Royal College of Physicians
## AT EDINBURGH,

FROM THE FIRST ERECTION OF THE COLLEGE, ON THE 29TH NOVEMBER 1681.

### LIST OF THOSE IN THE ORIGINAL PATENT.

| | |
|---|---|
| DAVID HAY. | ALEXANDER CRANSTONE. |
| THOMAS BURNET. | JOHN HUTTON. |
| MATTHEW BRISBAINE. | JOHN M'GILL. |
| ARCHIBALD STEVENSONE. | JOHN LERMONTH. |
| ROBERT SIBBALD. | WILLIAM STEVENSONE. |
| JAMES LIVINGSTONE. | JAMES HALKET. |
| ANDREW BALFOURE. | WILLIAM WRIGHT. |
| ROBERT CRAWFURD. | PATRICK HALYBURTON. |
| ROBERT TROTTER. | WILLIAM LAUDER. |
| MATTHEW SINCLARE. | ARCHIBALD PITCAIRNE. |
| JAMES STEWART. | |

### LIST OF FELLOWS ADMITTED.

| Names of Fellows. | Dates of their Diplomas. | Places where they received their Degrees. | Dates of their Licences to Practise. | Dates of their admission as Fellows. |
|---|---|---|---|---|
| PETER KELLO | ... | ... | ... | Dec. 11, 1682 |
| JOHN ABERNETHY | June 9, 1683 | Orange | Aug. 13, 1684 | Dec. 4, 1684 |
| *From this to the year 1693, the Record is wanting; but, from subsequent sederunts, it appears that, during this period, there were admitted—* | | | | |
| WILLIAM STEVENSON, WILLIAM ECCLES. WILLIAM DOUGLAS THOMAS SPENCE. ROBERT HAY. | | | | |

## List of Fellows.

| Names of Fellows. | Dates of their Diplomas. | Places where they received their Degrees. | Dates of their Licences to Practise. | Dates of their admission as Fellows. |
|---|---|---|---|---|
| CHARLES OLIPHANT | ... | ... | May 15, 1693 | Nov. 9, 1693 |
| ANDREW MELVILLE | 1683 | Caen, in Normandy. | July 5, 1694 | July 5, 1694 |
| JOSEPH DALRYMPLE | ... | ... | ... | July 30, 1694 |
| JAMES ROBERTSON | ... | ... | ... | Sept. 27, 1694 |
| DAVID DICKSON | Feb. 21, 1690 | Harderwick | Oct. 8, 1694 | Oct. 8, 1694 |
| GEORGE STIRLING | ... | ... | Oct. 16, 1694 | Oct. 16, 1694 |
| JOHN SMELLOME | ... | ... | Oct. 23, 1694 | Oct. 23, 1694 |
| GEORGE HEPBURN | ... | ... | Nov. 15, 1694 | Nov. 15, 1694 |
| ROBERT CARMICHAEL | July 1, 1694 | Leyden | Dec. 3, 1694 | Dec. 3, 1694 |
| DAVID MITCHELL | ... | ... | ... | Sept. 14, 1695 |
| SIR EDWARD EIZAT | | | | |
| WILL. BLACKADDER | ... | ... | ... | Sept. 16, 1695 |
| GILBERT RULE | ... | ... | ... | Oct. 2, 1695 |
| ADAM FREER | ... | Leyden | Oct. 7, 1695 | Oct. 7, 1695 |
| ALEXANDER DUNDAS | ... | ... | Nov. 4, 1695 | Nov. 4, 1695 |
| JAMES FORREST | June 12, 1691 | Leyden | Nov. 20, 1696 | Nov. 20, 1696 |
| WILLIAM JARDINE | March 25, 1697 | Harderwick | April 27, 1698 | April 28, 1698 |
| JOHN HAY | Jan. 21, 1701 | Aberdeen | Nov. 16, 1702 | Nov. 19, 1702 |
| JOHN RIDDELL | ... | ... | Nov. 26, 1702 | Nov. 26, 1702 |
| JOHN ST CLAIR | | | | |
| JOHN MONRO | ... | Aberdeen | Jan. 7, 1704 | Jan. 7, 1704 |
| JOHN DRUMMOND | ... | Aberdeen | | |
| JAMES LUITFOOT | ... | Orange | Feb. 9, 1704 | Feb. 9, 1704 |
| WILLIAM LERMONT | ... | Rheims | Feb. 9, 1704 | Feb. 9, 1704 |
| WILLIAM STEWART | July 24, 1704 | St Andrews | July 28, 1704 | Aug. 15, 1704 |
| FRANCIS PRINGLE | July 14, 1702 | Leyden | Nov. 21, 1704 | Dec. 1, 1704 |
| CHARLES PRESTON | ... | ... | | |
| GEORGE MACKENZIE | ... | ... | | |
| DAVID COCKBURN | May 14, 1705 | Edinburgh | June 29, 1705 | Aug. 30, 1705 |
| JAMES BROWN | April 12, 1704 | Rheims | Feb. 25, 1706 | Aug. 12, 1707 |
| WILL. ALEXANDER | July 23, 1699 | Rheims | June 18, 1706 | |
| PATRICK SINCLAIR | Oct. 24, 1703 | Utrecht | Nov. 14, 1706 | Aug. 12, 1707 |
| THOMAS YOUNG | June 18, 1694 | Utrecht | Sept. 23, 1707 | Dec. 12, 1707 |
| ROBERT LOWIS | Oct. 29, 1707 | Leyden | Sept. 7, 1708 | Nov. 9, 1708 |
| JAMES CRAWFORD | July 6, 1707 | Leyden | Dec. 12, 1710 | Feb. 13, 1711 |
| NIC. MONTGOMERIE | July 30, 1708 | Rheims | Dec. 29, 1709 | Aug. 5, 1712 |
| JOHN MENZIES | July 8, 1709 | Utrecht | May 6, 1712 | Dec. 10, 1712 |
| WILLIAM ARTHUR | March 12, 1707 | Utrecht | Feb. 9, 1714 | June 1, 1714 |
| GEORGE PATULLO | April 23, 1710 | Rheims | March 23, 1714 | June 15, 1714 |
| JOHN CLERK | July 5, 1711 | St Andrews | June 15, 1714 | Dec. 14, 1714 |
| WILLIAM HAMILTON | Aug. 15, 1711 | Harderwick | June 15, 1714 | Dec. 14, 1714 |
| WILLIAM COCHRAN | Aug. 4, 1712 | Rheims | Jan. 7, 1715 | Aug. 2, 1715 |
| ROBERT THOMSON | July 15, 1713 | Rheims | June 5, 1716 | Aug. 1, 1716 |
| JOHN BURNET | Aug. 7, 1719 | Edinburgh | Aug. 10, 1719 | Aug. 10, 1719 |
| JAMES ECCLES | Nov. 10, 1718 | Edinburgh | March 24, 1719 | Sept. 29, 1719 |
| JOHN LERMONT | Sept. 12, 1713 | Rheims | Nov. 10, 1719 | Nov. 1, 1720 |
| JOHN MARSHALL | Oct. 22, 1719 | Aberdeen | Mar. 21, 1721 | Aug. 1, 1721 |

## List of Fellows.

| Names of Fellows. | Dates of their Diplomas. | Places where they received their Degrees. | Dates of their Licences to Practise. | Dates of their Admission as Fellows. |
|---|---|---|---|---|
| CHARLES ALSTON | Dec. 2, 1719 | Glasgow | April 13, 1721 | Aug. 1 1721 |
| WILL. PORTERFIELD | Aug. 24, 1717 | Rheims | June 8, 1721 | Nov. 14, 1721 |
| DAVID KINNEIR | June 12, 1714 | St Andrews | Aug. 23, 1723 | Feb. 4, 1724 |
| GEORGE OSWALD | Aug. 11, 1696 / Nov. 16, 1723 | Rheims / Edinburgh | Nov. 21, 1723 | Feb. 4, 1724 |
| JOHN RUTHERFORD | July 21, 1719 | Rheims | March 24, 1724 | Nov. 3, 1724 |
| ANDREW SINCLAIR | July 10, 1720 | Angers | Feb. 25, 1724 | Nov. 3, 1724 |
| ANDREW PLUMBER | July 23, 1722 | Leyden | Feb. 25, 1724 | Nov. 3, 1724 |
| JOHN INNES | Nov. 21, 1722 | Padua | March 24, 1724 | Nov. 3, 1724 |
| ALEXANDER SCOTT | July 22, 1713 / Oct. 2, 1724 | Rheims / St Andrews | Feb. 9, 1725 | Feb. 9, 1725 |
| JAMES DUNDAS | Aug. 22, 1722 | Rheims | March 2, 1725 | Nov. 2, 1725 |
| SIR ALEX. DICK | Aug. 31, 1725 / Jan. 23, 1727 | Leyden / St Andrews | Feb. 7, 1727 | Nov. 7, 1727 |
| JOHN STEVENSON | Jan. 1710 | Harderwick | May 6, 1729 | Aug. 5, 1729 |
| JOHN TAYLOR | Mar. 21, 1727 / July 4, 1727 | Glasgow / St Andrews | Aug. 5, 1729 | Aug. 4, 1730 |
| CHARLES NISBET | Oct. 2, 1733 | St Andrews | Jan. 3, 1734 | Feb. 4, 1735 |
| JOHN PRINGLE | July 20, 1739 | Leyden | Aug. 27, 1734 | |
| DAVID FOULIS | Oct. 10, 1735 | Rheims | Jan. 18, 1737 | Aug. 2, 1737 |
| JAMES BAIRD | Aug. 21, 1733 / June 3, 1737 | Rheims / St Andrews | June 21, 1737 | May 2, 1738 |
| ROBERT WHYTT | April 2, 1736 / Oct. 31, 1737 | Rheims / St Andrews | Dec. 13, 1737 | Nov. 7, 1738 |
| BERNARD ALLAN | May 11, 1742 | St Andrews | Nov. 2, 1742 | Nov. 2, 1742 |
| ADAM MURRAY | Dec. 19, 1726 | St Andrews | Aug. 13, 1743 | Aug. 13, 1743 |
| SIR STUART THREIPLAND | Aug. 9, 1742 | Edinburgh | May 3, 1743 | Feb. 7, 1744 |
| JOHN COCHRANE | May 5, 1744 | St Andrews | May 15, 1744 | May 15, 1744 |
| ALEX. CAMPBELL | April 30, 1746 | St Andrews | May 6, 1746 | May 6, 1746 |
| THOMAS LIDDERDALE | Oct. 20, 1747 | St Andrews | Feb. 2, 1748 | Feb. 2, 1748 |
| JOHN BOSWELL | Nov. 1, 1736 | Leyden | Sept. 13, 1737 | Aug. 2, 1748 |
| DAVID CLERK | Aug. 15, 1746 | Edinburgh | Nov. 1, 1748 | Nov. 7, 1749 |
| JOHN STEUART | March 12, 1740 | Rheims | Aug. 5, 1746 | May 1, 1750 |
| JAMES LIND | May 3, 1748 | Edinburgh | Aug. 2, 1748 | May 1, 1750 |
| THOMAS ELLIOT | Aug. 15, 1746 | Edinburgh | Nov. 7, 1749 | Feb. 5, 1751 |
| COLIN DRUMMOND | Aug. 22, 1750 | Edinburgh | Feb. 5, 1751 | May 5, 1752 |
| FRANCIS HOME | March 7, 1750 | Edinburgh | May 7, 1751 | Aug. 4, 1752 |
| WILLIAM CUMMING | April 6, 1750 / July 9, 1752 | Rheims / Edinburgh | Aug. 4, 1752 | Aug. 4, 1752 |
| ALEX. STEVENSON | July 12, 1749 | Glasgow | Nov. 5, 1751 | Feb. 6, 1753 |
| JAMES GRIEVE | 1733 | Edinburgh | Feb. 6, 1753 | |
| JOHN FOTHERGILL | Aug. 13, 1736 | Edinburgh | Aug. 6, 1754 | Aug. 6, 1754 |
| WILLIAM CULLEN | Sept. 14, 1740 | Glasgow | Feb. 3, 1756 | March 5, 1756 |
| ALEXANDER MUNRO | Jan. 1, 1756 | Edinburgh | | |
| PATRICK HALDANE | Aug. 3, 1758 | St Andrews | Aug. 10, 1758 | Aug. 10, 1758 |
| NORTH VIGOR | June 12, 1747 | Edinburgh | Nov. 7, 1758 | Nov. 7, 1758 |
| GREGORY GRANT | May 4, 1753 / May 4, 1754 | Rheims / Aberdeen | Nov. 1, 1757 | Nov. 7, 1758 |

## List of Fellows.

| Names of Fellows. | Dates of their Diplomas. | Places where they received their Degrees. | Dates of their Licences to Practise. | Dates of their admission as Fellows. |
|---|---|---|---|---|
| ALEX. MUNRO, Jun. | Oct. 25, 1755 | Edinburgh | May 2, 1758 | May 1, 1759 |
| WILLIAM BAYLIES | Dec. 18, 1748 | Aberdeen | Aug. 7, 1759 | Aug. 7, 1759 |
| THOMAS GLEN | { July 31, 1726 <br> July 27, 1730 | Rheims <br> St Andrews } | Nov. 6. 1759 | May 6, 1760 |
| ROBERT RAMSAY | Dec. 10, 1757 | Edinburgh | Dec. 11, 1759 | } May 5, 1761 |
| EDWARD WRIGHT | June 15, 1753 | Edinburgh | Feb. 5, 1760 | |
| JOHN GARDINER | Dec. 29, 1759 | Edinburgh | Aug. 5, 1760 | Aug. 4, 1761 |
| JOHN HOPE | Jan. 29, 1750 | Glasgow | Nov. 6, 1750 | Feb. 2, 1762 |
| ADAM AUSTIN | May 15, 1749 | Glasgow | Aug. 7, 1753 | Aug. 3, 1762 |
| THOMAS YOUNG | Nov. 30, 1761 | Edinburgh | Dec. 8, 1761 | Nov. 2, 1762 |
| WILLIAM BUTTER | Sept. 16, 1761 | Edinburgh | Aug. 2, 1763 | Nov. 1, 1763 |
| JAMES WALKER | May 28, 1752 | St Andrews } | Nov. 1, 1763 | Feb. 7, 1764 |
| JAMES GRAINGER | March 14, 1753 | Edinburgh } | | |
| THOMAS LIVINGSTONE | Dec. 1752 | Aberdeen } | Feb. 7, 1764 | May 1, 1764 |
| ROBERT PETRIE | May 30, 1750 | Edinburgh } | | |
| ANDREW WILSON | June 29, 1749 | Edinburgh | Aug. 7, 1764 | } Nov. 6, 1764 |
| MAXWELL GARTSHORE | May 8, 1764 | Edinburgh | June 12, 1764 | |
| JOHN GREGORY | March 13, 1746 | Aberdeen } | March 5, 1765 | Aug. 6, 1765 |
| JOHN MORGAN | July 18, 1763 | Edinburgh } | | |
| JOHN STEEDMAN | Nov. 15, 1740 | Rheims | Aug. 7, 1764 | Nov. 5, 1765 |
| JAMES HAY | Nov. 8, 1758 | St Andrews | Feb. 5, 1765 | Aug. 5, 1766 |
| JOSEPH BLACK | June 11, 1754 | Edinburgh | Feb. 3, 1767 | May 5, 1767 |
| ARTHUR NICOLSON | March 10, 1763 | Aberdeen | May 5, 1767 | Aug. 4, 1767 |
| JAMES M'KITTRICK | Sept. 12, 1766 | Edinburgh | Aug. 4, 1767 | Nov. 3, 1767 |
| WILLIAM SHIPPEN, Jun. | Sept. 16, 1761 | Edinburgh | Nov. 3, 1767 | Feb. 2, 1768 |
| WILL. MACFARLANE | { Aug. 8, 1725 <br> March 15, 1727 | Rheims <br> St Andrews } | Nov. 7, 1727 | Dec. 12. 1768 |
| JAMES SPENCE | Sept. 4, 1764 | St Andrews | March 30, 1769 | Aug. 1, 1769 |
| JAMES AIKMAN | July 6, 1768 | Aberdeen | Feb. 7, 1769 | May 1, 1770 |
| JAMES LIND | Sept. 12, 1768 | Edinburgh | Nov. 7, 1769 | Nov. 6, 1770 |
| ANDREW DUNCAN | Oct. 25, 1769 | St Andrews | May 1, 1770 | May 7, 1771 |
| GEORGE TAILOUR | Jan. 27, 1768 | Glasgow | Feb. 5, 1771 | May 7, 1771 |
| MARTIN ECCLES | Aug. 21, 1753 | St Andrews | June 20, 1771 | Nov. 5, 1771 |
| WILLIAM BUCHAN | June 2, 1761 | Edinburgh | Aug. 6, 1771 | Nov. 5, 1772 |
| JAMES HAMILTON | June 12, 1771 | Edinburgh | Nov. 5, 1771 | Nov. 3, 1772 |
| NATHANIEL SPENS | June 4, 1773 | St Andrews | Aug. 3, 1773 | July 7, 1774 |
| ROBERT HAMILTON | May 12, 1766 | St Andrews | Nov. 3, 1773 | Feb. 1, 1774 |
| EDWARD SPRY | Jan. 4, 1759 | Aberdeen | Feb. 1, 1774 | May 3, 1774 |
| JAMES HUNTER | June 2, 1747 | St Andrews | Feb. 24, 1774 | July 14, 1774 |
| ROBERT LANGLANDS | July 4, 1750 | Edinburgh | May 2, 1775 | May 7, 1776 |
| DANIEL RUTHERFORD | Sept. 12, 1772 | Edinburgh | Feb. 6, 1776 | May 6, 1777 |
| JAMES GREGORY | June 18, 1774 | Edinburgh | Feb. 6, 1776 | May 6, 1777 |
| ARNOLD B. BEEREN-BROK | } June 24, 1774 | Leyden | Aug. 11, 1777 | Feb. 3, 1778 |
| MATTHEW POWELL | Aug. 27, 1773 | St Andrews | Nov. 4, 1777 | Aug. 4, 1778 |
| JAMES HAMILTON | Aug. 13, 1771 | Aberdeen | Nov. 2, 1779 | Feb. 1, 1780 |
| WILLIAM WRIGHT | Oct. 25, 1763 | St Andrews | Feb. 1, 1780 | May 2, 1780 |
| THOMAS GILLESPIE | Dec. 1, 1766 | Aberdeen | Nov. 2, 1779 | Nov. 7, 1780 |

## List of Fellows.

| Names of Fellows. | Dates of their Diplomas. | Places where they received their Degrees. | Dates of their Licences to Practise. | Dates of their Admission as Fellows. |
|---|---|---|---|---|
| THOMAS MEIK | May 11, 1772 | St Andrews | Feb. 6, 1781 | May 1, 1781 |
| JOHN LIND | Jan. 4, 1777 | St Andrews | Feb. 6, 1781 | May 1, 1781 |
| WILLIAM GRIEVE | Sept. 12, 1770 | Edinburgh | May 1, 1781 | May 7, 1782 |
| HENRY CULLEN | June 24, 1780 | Edinburgh | Aug. 6, 1782 | Nov. 5, 1782 |
| JOHN ELLISON | Nov. 30, 1782 | St Andrews | May 6, 1783 | Aug. 5, 1783 |
| ROBERT STEVENSON | June 24, 1778 | Edinburgh | Aug. 5, 1783 | Nov. 4, 1783 |
| JOHN JOSEPH SUE | Aug. 26, 1783 | St Andrews | Sept. 1, 1783 | Nov. 4, 1783 |
| JOHN MARSHALL | Aug. 26, 1783 | St Andrews | Nov. 4, 1783 | Dec. 4, 1783 |
| JAMES WOOD | Sept. 12, 1776 | Edinburgh | Feb. 3, 1784 | May 4, 1784 |
| ROBERT GRANT | Aug. 24, 1780 | Aberdeen | May 4, 1784 | Aug. 3, 1784 |
| ANDW. FARQUHARSON | Oct. 27, 1784 | St Andrews | Nov. 2, 1784 | Feb. 1, 1785 |
| THOMAS KERR | Nov. 25, 1784 | Aberdeen | Dec. 2, 1784 | Feb. 1, 1785 |
| JOHN CLARK | June 7, 1773 | St Andrews | March 23, 1785 | May 3, 1785 |
| WILL. FARQUHARSON | Sept. 28, 1778 | Aberdeen | March 23, 1785 | May 3, 1785 |
| JAMES CAMPBELL | Oct. 17, 1781 | St Andrews | Nov. 1, 1785 | Feb. 7, 1786 |
| HENRY M'LAGGAN | Sept. 20, 1784 | Glasgow | Nov. 1, 1785 | Feb. 7, 1786 |
| ROBERT FREER | Feb. 23, 1779 | Aberdeen | Feb. 7, 1786 | May 2, 1786 |
| DAVID MORTON | Sept. 1, 1768 | Aberdeen | May 2, 1786 | Aug. 1, 1786 |
| THOMAS STEVENSON | July 24, 1786 | St Andrews | Aug. 1, 1786 | Nov. 7, 1786 |
| THOMAS COCHRANE | Nov. 27, 1784 | Glasgow | Nov. 7, 1786 | Nov. 6, 1787 |
| SAMUEL SPALDING | Sept. 26, 1785 | St Andrews | May 1, 1787 | Aug. 7, 1787 |
| GEO. BACHMATIEV | Sept. 12, 1786 | Edinburgh | Aug. 7, 1787 | Aug. 21, 1787 |
| THOMAS SPENS | Sept. 13, 1784 | Edinburgh | Nov. 6, 1787 | Feb. 5, 1788 |
| JOHN DRUMMOND | June 8, 1786 | St Andrews | Nov. 6, 1787 | Feb. 5, 1788 |
| PAT. BARON SETON | Sept. 12, 1787 | Edinburgh | Nov. 6, 1787 | Feb. 5, 1788 |
| WILLIAM SPINK | Aug. 1, 1788 | St Andrews | Aug. 5, 1788 | Aug. 19, 1788 |
| CHARLES STUART | Sept. 12, 1781 | Edinburgh | March 4, 1783 | Feb. 3, 1789 |
| ALEX. HAMILTON | Mar. 19, 1783 | St Andrews | Feb. 5, 1788 | Feb. 3, 1789 |
| ALEX. GRANT CLUGSTON | Sept. 6, 1788 | St Andrews | Jan. 13, 1789 | Feb. 3, 1789 |
| JOHN CRAIGIE | Dec. 27, 1788 | Aberdeen | Jan. 13, 1789 | Feb. 3, 1789 |
| CHARLES WEBSTER | Sept. 12, 1777 | Edinburgh | Feb. 1, 1780 | May 5, 1789 |
| CHARLES CONGALTON | April 4, 1771 | St Andrews | Feb. 5, 1788 | May 5, 1789 |
| THOMAS GILLIES | July 28, 1768 | Aberdeen | May 5, 1789 | Aug. 3, 1789 |
| JAMES CLARK | Sept. 17, 1773 | Aberdeen | May 5, 1789 | Aug. 3, 1789 |
| WILLIAM ROXBURGH | Jan. 12, 1790 | Aberdeen | Feb. 2, 1790 | Feb. 13, 1790 |
| GEORGE WILSON | Jan. 2, 1790 | Aberdeen | Aug. 3, 1790 | Nov. 3, 1790 |
| JOHN LORIMER | April 29, 1764 | St Andrews | May 3, 1791 | Aug. 2, 1791 |
| WIL. MONCRIEFF | Sept. 12, 1768 | Edinburgh | June 1, 1791 | ... |
| ANDREW FILLAN | May 4, 1791 | Aberdeen | June 1, 1791 | Aug. 2, 1791 |
| JAMES HOME | Sept. 18, 1781 | Edinburgh | Feb. 1, 1791 | Nov. 1, 1791 |
| JAMES CURRIE | Mar. 30, 1780 | Glasgow | Aug. 2, 1791 | ... |
| JO. COAKLEY LETSOM | June 20, 1769 | Leyden | Oct. 25, 1791 | Dec. 1, 1791 |
| NICOLAS BINDON | Sept. 12, 1788 | Edinburgh | Nov. 1, 1791 | ... |
| THOMAS ARNOLD | Nov. 29, 1766 | Edinburgh | Nov. 24, 1791 | ... |
| JOHN YULE | Sept. 12, 1785 | Edinburgh | ... | ... |
| JOSEPH FOX | Feb. 1, 1783 | St Andrews | Feb. 7, 1792 | Mar. 6, 1792 |
| JAMES M'DONNELY | Sept. 13, 1784 | Edinburgh | ... | ... |
| JAMES HAMILTON, Jun. | Feb. 8, 1792 | St Andrews | Feb. 17, 1792 | Mar. 6, 1792 |

## List of Fellows.

| Names of Fellows. | Dates of their Diplomas. | Places where they received their Degrees. | Dates of their Licences to Practise. | Dates of their admission as Fellows. |
|---|---|---|---|---|
| ANDREW YOUNG | June 22, 1793 | Aberdeen | Aug. 22, 1793 | Nov. 5, 1793 |
| JAMES M'KITTRICK ADAIR | Sept. 12, 1789 | Edinburgh | Nov. 15, 1792 | Dec. 5, 1793 |
| ANGUS M'DONALD | Jan. 10, 1789 | St Andrews | Dec. 5, 1793 | Feb. 3, 1794 |
| ALEX. PHILIP WILSON | June 25, 1792 | Edinburgh | Feb. 3, 1794 | Feb. 3, 1795 |
| JAMES BUCHAN | Sept. 12, 1792 | Edinburgh | Aug. 5, 1794 | Aug. 4, 1795 |
| JAMES GASKING | June 10, 1789 | Leyden | Oct. 27, 1795 | Feb. 2, 1796 |
| ALEX. STEWART | Nov. 2, 1795 | St Andrews | Dec. 3, 1795 | Feb. 2, 1796 |
| SIR WALTER FARQUHAR, Bart. | Jan. 19, 1796 | Aberdeen | March 1, 1796 | May 3, 1796 |
| JO. HUTTON COOPER | Mar. 1, 1796 | St Andrews | March 15, 1796 | ... |
| SIR ALEX. DOUGLAS, Bart. | July 11, 1760 | St Andrews | May 10, 1796 | May 18, 1796 |
| THO. CHA. HOPE | Sept. 12, 1787 | Edinburgh | Nov. 5, 1795 | Nov. 1, 1796 |
| GEORGE DICKSON | Aug. 8, 1796 | St Andrews | Sept. 6, 1796 | Dec. 1, 1796 |
| ANDREW DUNCAN | Sept. 12, 1794 | Edinburgh | Nov. 1, 1796 | ... |
| ANDREW KELTIE | ... | Aberdeen | ... | ... |
| ALEX. MONRO | Sept. 12, 1797 | Edinburgh | Nov. 5, 1797 | Nov. 30, 1797 |
| COLIN LAUDER | July 24, 1786 | St Andrews | Nov. 30, 1797 | May 1, 1798 |
| GEO. GAVIN BROWN | Aug. 22, 1797 | St Andrews | Dec. 6, 1798 | May 7, 1799 |
| ALEXANDER WILSON | Dec. 17, 1796 | St Andrews | Feb. 5, 1799 | ... |
| MATTHEW POOLE | Aug. 18, 1798 | St Andrews | Aug. 6, 1799 | Nov. 5, 1799 |
| ROBERT KENNEDY | Sept. 12, 1794 | Edinburgh | May 7, 1799 | Aug. 5, 1800 |
| WILLIAM KENNEDY | April 12, 1800 | Aberdeen | Aug. 5, 1800 | Nov. 4, 1800 |
| THOMAS JAMIESON | Jan. 15, 1791 | Aberdeen | Dec. 5, 1799 | Nov. 4, 1800 |
| NICOLAS ROMAYNE | June 24, 1780 | Edinburgh | Aug. 28, 1800 | Nov. 4, 1800 |
| SIR ALEX. MORISON | Sept. 12, 1799 | Edinburgh | May 6, 1800 | May 11, 1801 |
| WILLIAM WARD | Sept. 12, 1800 | Edinburgh | Feb. 3, 1801 | May 5, 1801 |
| JAMES ROBERTSON | Oct. 14, 1794 | Aberdeen | March 30, 1802 | May 4, 1802 |
| DONALD SMITH | May 6, 1785 | St Andrews | May 3, 1803 | Aug. 2, 1803 |
| OSWALD HUNTER | June 24, 1803 | Edinburgh | Aug. 2, 1803 | Nov. 1, 1803 |
| WILLIAM DICK | Feb. 24, 1803 | Aberdeen | June 1, 1804 | Nov. 6, 1804 |
| WILLIAM FRANKLIN | July 7, 1795 | Aberdeen | Aug. 7, 1804 | Nov. 6, 1804 |
| ROBINSON FOXLEY | Oct. 8, 1804 | St Andrews | Feb. 5, 1805 | May 7, 1805 |
| JOHN GRAY | May 11, 1805 | Aberdeen | Aug. 6, 1805 | Nov. 5, 1805 |
| SAMUEL M'DOWELL | June 14, 1805 | St Andrews | Aug. 6, 1805 | Nov. 5, 1805 |
| THOMAS BROWN | Sept. 12, 1803 | Edinburgh | Feb. 5, 1805 | Feb. 4, 1806 |
| ALEX. MACKENZIE | Mar. 13, 1803 | St Andrews | May 6, 1806 | Aug. 5, 1806 |
| JOHN BARCLAY | June 24, 1796 | Edinburgh | Nov. 5, 1805 | Nov. 4, 1806 |
| WILLIAM WIGHTMAN | June 3, 1790 | St Andrews | Aug. 5, 1806 | Nov. 4, 1806 |
| JAMES MACGREGOR | Feb. 17, 1804 | Aberdeen | Nov. 26, 1806 | May 5, 1807 |
| GEORGE ALLEY | April 11, 1807 | St Andrews | Nov. 3, 1807 | Feb. 2, 1808 |
| WILLIAM GOURLAY | June 24, 1782 | Edinburgh | Feb. 2, 1808 | May 3, 1808 |
| THOMAS GRAY | April 7, 1800 | Aberdeen | Aug. 2, 1808 | Nov. 1, 1808 |
| JOSHUA H. DAVIDSON | June 24, 1807 | Edinburgh | Aug. 2, 1808 | Aug. 1, 1809 |
| ALEXANDER WYLIE | July 2, 1808 | St Andrews | Nov. 1, 1808 | Nov. 7, 1809 |
| ADAM BURT | March 26, 1808 | St Andrews | Aug. 1, 1809 | Nov. 7, 1809 |
| JOHN CHEYNE | June 24, 1795 | Edinburgh | Feb. 22, 1810 | May 1, 1810 |

## List of Fellows.

| Names of Fellows. | Dates of their Diplomas. | Places where they received their Degrees. | Dates of their Licences to Practise. | Dates of their admission as Fellows. |
|---|---|---|---|---|
| JAMES MUTTLEBURY | April 21, 1810 | St Andrews | May 1, 1810 | Aug. 7, 1810 |
| JAMES PROUD JOHNSON | Sept. 23, 1805 | St Andrews | Aug. 7, 1810 | Nov. 6, 1810 |
| HENRY HARDIE | Sept. 12, 1809 | Edinburgh | Feb. 5, 1811 | May 7, 1811 |
| JAMES ANDERSON | Sept. 21, 1810 | Aberdeen | Nov. 6, 1810 | Nov. 5, 1811 |
| DAVID DANIEL DAVIS | May 4, 1801 | Glasgow | Feb. 4, 1812 | May 5, 1812 |
| JOHN BIGSBY | June 2, 1810 | St Andrews | Feb. 4, 1812 | May 5, 1812 |
| WIL. ELFORD LEACH | Jan. 18, 1812 | St Andrews | Feb. 4, 1812 | May 5, 1812 |
| WILLIAM FERGUSON | March 21, 1812 | St Andrews | May 5, 1812 | Aug. 4, 1812 |
| WIL. PULTENEY ALISON | Sept. 12, 1811 | Edinburgh | Nov. 5, 1811 | Nov. 3, 1812 |
| ALEX. MACLARTY | Sept. 12, 1795 | Edinburgh | Feb. 1, 1813 | May 4, 1813 |
| BENJAMIN BARTLET BUCHANAN | Sept. 12, 1808 | Edinburgh | Aug. 4, 1812 | Aug. 3, 1813 |
| JOHN WARROCH PURSELL | Sept. 12, 1798 | Edinburgh | March 2, 1810 | Aug. 3, 1813 |
| JOHN CLARK | Aug. 5, 1806 / Aug. 1, 1821 | St Andrews / Edinburgh | March 2, 1813 | Aug. 3, 1813 |
| WILLIAM MAXTON | Sept. 22, 1804 | St Andrews | Nov. 2, 1813 | Feb. 1, 1814 |
| JOHN WILLIAMSON | Oct. 20, 1813 | St Andrews | Nov. 2, 1813 | Feb. 1, 1814 |
| SAMUEL FERGUSSON | Nov. 6, 1813 | St Andrews | Dec. 2, 1813 | May 3, 1814 |
| ROBERT BRIGGS | Sept. 12, 1806 | St Andrews | Dec. 18, 1813 | May 3, 1814 |
| JOHN BOWEN | Oct. 9, 1809 | St Andrews | Feb. 1, 1814 | May 3, 1814 |
| BENJAMIN LARA | May 17, 1802 | Aberdeen | Feb. 12, 1814 | Aug. 2, 1814 |
| GEORGE MAGRATH | Aug. 3, 1805 | St Andrews | Aug. 2, 1814 | Nov. 1, 1814 |
| WILLIAM BEATTY | Feb. 28, 1806 | Aberdeen | Aug. 2, 1814 | Nov. 1, 1814 |
| HENRY DEWAR | June 25, 1804 | Edinburgh | Feb. 1, 1814 | Feb. 7, 1815 |
| ANTHONY LINDSAY | Dec. 16, 1814 | Aberdeen | Feb. 7, 1815 | May 2, 1815 |
| JAMES MURDOCH | July 9, 1814 | St Andrews | Aug. 2, 1814 | Aug. 1, 1815 |
| ANDREW NICOLL | Sept. 12, 1810 | Edinburgh | May 2, 1815 | Aug. 1, 1815 |
| JOHN MURRAY | Oct. 17, 1814 | St Andrews | Nov. 1, 1814 | Nov. 7, 1815 |
| GEORGE DRYSDALE | June 1, 1815 | St Andrews | July 15, 1815 | Nov. 7, 1815 |
| HEN. EVANS HOLDER | Aug. 24, 1801 | St Andrews | Nov. 7, 1815 | Feb. 6, 1610 |
| WILLIAM PYM | April 2, 1799 | St Andrews | Feb. 6, 1816 | May 7, 1816 |
| DAVID AIRD | Sept. 12, 1805 | Edinburgh | Feb. 6, 1816 | May 7, 1816 |
| ISAAC WILSON | Dec. 23, 1796 | St Andrews | May 7, 1816 | Aug. 6, 1816 |
| DAVID JAMES HAMILTON DICKSON | Aug. 18, 1806 | Aberdeen | May 7, 1816 | Aug. 6, 1816 |
| ROBERT JOHN HUME | Jan. 12, 1816 | St Andrews | Aug. 6, 1816 | Nov. 5, 1816 |
| JAMES CLARK | Feb. 7, 1817 | Aberdeen | Feb. 25, 1817 | Aug. 5, 1817 |
| WALTER OGILVIE | Apr. 14, 1817 | St Andrews | May 6, 1817 | Aug. 5, 1817 |
| WILLIAM WYNNE | Dec. 7, 1816 | St Andrews | May 6, 1817 | Aug. 5, 1817 |
| JOHN RAMSAY | Sept. 12, 1810 | Edinburgh | May 16, 1817 | Nov. 4, 1817 |
| PAT. CAMPBELL BAIRD | Mar. 7, 1818 | St Andrews | May 5, 1818 | Aug. 4, 1818 |
| WILL. MONCRIEFF | June 24, 1814 | Edinburgh | Nov. 4, 1817 | Nov. 3, 1818 |
| SAMUEL SPROULE | July 4, 1818 | St Andrews | Aug. 4, 1818 | Nov. 3, 1818 |
| WM. PRESTON LAUDER | Mar. 4, 1809 | St Andrews | May 5, 1818 | May 4, 1819 |
| ANDREW KENNEY | June 24, 1812 | Edinburgh | May 5, 1818 | May 4, 1819 |
| JAMES THOS. BROWN WATT | June 24, 1809 | Edinburgh | Dec. 19, 1818 | May 4, 1819 |

## List of Fellows.

| Names of Fellows. | Dates of their Diplomas. | Places where they received their Degrees. | Dates of their Licences to Practise. | Dates of their admission as Fellows. |
|---|---|---|---|---|
| WALTER ADAM | Aug. 1, 1816 | Edinburgh | Nov. 3, 1818 | Nov. 2, 1819 |
| AUGUSTUS WEST | Dec. 5, 1818 | St Andrews | Aug. 3, 1819 | Nov. 2, 1819 |
| EDWARD TURNER | Aug. 2, 1819 | Edinburgh | Aug. 3, 1819 | Nov. 2, 1819 |
| ALEX. KENNEDY | Jan. 30, 1819 | Aberdeen | Mar. 3, 1819 | May 2, 1820 |
| JAMES MILLAR | June 24, 1795 | Edinburgh | May 4, 1819 | May 2, 1820 |
| STEPH. MACMULLEN | Jan. 7, 1815 | St Andrews | Feb. 1, 1820 | May 2, 1820 |
| JAMES GILLIES | May 13, 1816 | Aberdeen | Feb. 1, 1820 | May 2, 1820 |
| Sir JAS. RO. GRANT | June 20, 1814 | Aberdeen | May 2, 1820 | Aug. 1, 1820 |
| EBENEZER GAIRDNER | Aug. 2, 1819 | Edinburgh | Aug. 1, 1820 | Nov. 7, 1820 |
| ROBERT GRAHAM | Sept. 12, 1808 | Edinburgh | Feb. 1, 1820 | Feb. 6, 1821 |
| JAMES GEORGE PLAYFAIR | Aug. 2, 1819 | Edinburgh | Feb. 1, 1820 | May 1, 1821 |
| JOHN BUTTER | Aug. 1, 1820 | Edinburgh | Aug. 7, 1821 | Nov. 6, 1821 |
| WILLIAM ARNOLD | Oct. 4, 1821 | Aberdeen | Nov. 6, 1821 | Feb. 5, 1822 |
| DAVID CAMPBELL | Jan. 18, 1771 | Leyden | Aug. 6, 1822 | Nov. 5, 1822 |
| ROBERT RENTON | June 24, 1814 | Edinburgh | Feb. 5, 1822 | Feb. 4, 1823 |
| Sir R. CHRISTISON, Bart. | Aug. 2, 1819 | Edinburgh | Feb. 5, 1822 | Feb. 4, 1823 |
| THOMAS KIDD | May 12, 1819 | Aberdeen | Aug. 6, 1822 | Feb. 4, 1823 |
| JOHN ABERCROMBIE | June 4, 1803 | Edinburgh | Aug. 6, 1822 | Aug. 4, 1823 |
| ROBERT GROAT | Sept. 12, 1783 | Edinburgh | Nov. 5, 1822 | Nov. 4, 1823 |
| G. AUGUSTUS BORTHWICK | June 24, 1808 | Edinburgh | Feb. 4, 1823 | Feb. 3, 1824 |
| ROBERT CARNEGY | Aug. 1, 1817 | Edinburgh | Feb. 4, 1823 | Feb. 3, 1824 |
| JOHN YOUNG | April 10, 1823 | Glasgow | May 6, 1823 | May 4, 1824 |
| THOMAS MAGRATH | June 3, 1809 | St Andrews | May 4, 1824 | Aug. 3, 1824 |
| WILLIAM BEILBY | Aug. 1, 1816 | Edinburgh | Aug. 4, 1823 | Nov. 2, 1824 |
| EDWARD MILLIGAN | Aug. 1, 1815 | Edinburgh | Nov. 4, 1823 | Nov. 2, 1824 |
| JOHN MACWHIRTER | Jan. 6, 1816 | St Andrews | Nov. 4, 1823 | Nov. 2, 1824 |
| THOMAS SHORTT | Aug. 1, 1815 | Edinburgh | Feb. 3, 1824 | Feb. 1, 1825 |
| JAMES WOOD | Sept. 12, 1809 | Edinburgh | May 4, 1824 | May 3, 1825 |
| ALEXANDER BOYLE | Aug. 28, 1812 | Aberdeen | Feb. 1, 1825 | May 3, 1825 |
| JOHN MURRAY | Feb. 5, 1825 | Aberdeen | May 3, 1825 | Aug. 2, 1825 |
| RICHARD POOLE | Feb. 16, 1803 | St Andrews | Nov. 2, 1824 | Nov. 1, 1825 |
| ROBERT GRANT | June 24, 1814 | Edinburgh | Dec. 28, 1825 | Feb. 6, 1827 |
| RICHARD HAWLEY | June 24, 1807 | Edinburgh | Feb. 7, 1826 | Feb. 6, 1827 |
| JAMES MELLIS | Jan. 4, 1806 | Aberdeen | Nov. 7, 1826 | Feb. 6, 1827 |
| Sir ANDW. HALLIDAY | June 24, 1806 | Edinburgh | Nov. 4, 1817 | Aug. 7, 1827 |
| JAMES MACDONALD | May 21, 1806 | St Andrews | Feb. 5, 1828 | May 6, 1828 |
| JOHN THATCHER | June 24, 1806 | Edinburgh | May 2, 1815 | May 6, 1828 |
| JAMES CRAWFURD GREGORY | Aug. 2, 1824 | Edinburgh | Nov. 6, 1827 | June 24, 1828 |
| PETER RAMSAY | Mar. 3, 1817 | St Andrews | June 24, 1828 | Nov. 4, 1828 |
| WILLIAM GREGORY | July 12, 1828 | Edinburgh | Aug. 5, 1828 | Aug. 4, 1829 |
| EDWARD DUFFIN ALLISON | Aug. 20, 1827 | Aberdeen | Jan. 13, 1829 | Feb. 2, 1830 |
| JOHN THOMSON | Jan. 11, 1808 | Aberdeen | Feb. 7, 1815 | Aug. 3, 1830 |
| JOHN PRICE | July 3, 1821 | Aberdeen | ... | Aug. 3, 1830 |
| ROBERT LEWINS | June 24, 1813 | Edinburgh | Nov. 3, 1829 | Nov. 2, 1830 |

## List of Fellows. 9

| Names of Fellows. | Dates of their Diplomas. | Places where they received their Degrees. | Dates of their admission as Fellows. |
|---|---|---|---|
| DAVID BOSWELL REID | July 12, 1830 | Edinburgh | Aug. 2, 1831 |
| JOHN MACKENZIE | Aug. 2, 1824 | Edinburgh | Nov. 1, 1831 |
| MONTGOMERY ROBERTSON | Oct. 16, 1829 | Aberdeen | Feb. 7, 1832 |
| ANDREW COMBE | Aug. 1, 1825 | Edinburgh | May 1, 1832 |
| JOHN HUME PEEBLES | Sept. 30, 1828 | Pisa | Aug. 7, 1832 |
| DAVID CRAIGIE | Aug. 1, 1816 | Edinburgh | Aug. 7, 1832 |
| PETER FAIRBAIRN | Aug. 2, 1819 | Edinburgh | Feb. 5, 1833 |
| THOS. STEWART TRAILL | Sept. 13, 1802 | Edinburgh | May 7, 1833 |
| ALEX. GEORGE HOME | Aug. 1, 1823 | Edinburgh | May 7, 1833 |
| JACOB D. HUNTER | July 12, 1831 | Edinburgh | May 7, 1833 |
| PATRICK CHARLES | July 12, 1828 | Edinburgh | Aug. 6, 1833 |
| WILLIAM GLOVER | Aug. 17, 1818 | St Andrews | Aug. 6, 1833 |
| WILLIAM THOMSON | Apr. 1, 1831 | Aberdeen | Oct. 12, 1833 |
| JOHN WILSON ANDERSON | Aug. 1, 1820 | Edinburgh | Oct. 12, 1833 |
| JOHN SMITH | Aug. 1, 1823 | Edinburgh | Oct. 12, 1833 |
| JAMES PATTERSON | July 12, 1832 | Edinburgh | Feb. 4, 1834 |
| J. D. MORRIES STIRLING | July 12, 1831 | Edinburgh | Feb. 4, 1834 |
| ROBERT SPITTAL | Mar. 11, 1832 | Giessen | May 6, 1834 |
| JAMES BURNES | Aug. 7, 1824 | St Andrews | Sept. 23, 1834 |
| CHARLES RANSFORD | July 12, 1833 | Edinburgh | Feb. 3, 1835 |
| RALPH RICHARDSON | Aug. 1, 1834 | Edinburgh | Feb. 3, 1835 |
| ARCHIBALD ROBERTSON | Aug. 1, 1817 | Edinburgh | Aug. 4, 1835 |
| THOS. B. HARNESS | Apr. 28, 1835 | St Andrews | Nov. 3, 1835 |
| WILLIAM MACDONALD | Aug. 1, 1818 | Edinburgh | Feb. 2, 1836 |
| SAMUEL HOBART | Aug. 30, 1835 | Erlangen | Feb. 2, 1836 |
| JOHN TILSTONE | Aug. 24, 1835 | Heidelberg | Aug. 2, 1836 |
| WILLIAM SELLER | Aug. 1, 1821 | Edinburgh | Oct. 4, 1836 |
| JOHN REID | July 12, 1830 | Edinburgh | Oct. 4, 1836 |
| Sir JAMES Y. SIMPSON, Bart. | July 12, 1832 | Edinburgh | Oct. 4, 1836 |
| HENRY ATKINSON | Aug. 1, 1835 | Erlangen | Oct. 4, 1836 |
| WILLIAM REID | Aug. 2, 1824 | Edinburgh | Feb. 7, 1837 |
| JOHN SPENS | Aug. 1, 1835 | Edinburgh | Feb. 7, 1837 |
| Sir JAMES COX | Aug. 1, 1835 | Edinburgh | Feb. 7, 1837 |
| CHARLES BELL | Apr. 27, 1836 | Glasgow | Feb. 7, 1837 |
| EDMUND B. LOCKYER | July 8, 1836 | Jena | Feb. 7, 1837 |
| MARTIN BARRY | July 12, 1833 | Edinburgh | July 15, 1837 |
| JOHN MOIR | July 12, 1828 | Edinburgh | July 15, 1837 |
| GEORGE PATERSON | July 12, 1833 | Edinburgh | July 15, 1837 |
| PATRICK ROLLAND | May 28, 1837 | Keil | July 15, 1837 |
| JOHN HOME | July 13, 1829 | Edinburgh | Feb. 6, 1838 |
| WILLIAM HENDERSON | July 12, 1831 | Edinburgh | Feb. 6, 1838 |
| JAMES MARR | Dec. 6, 1837 | St Andrews | Feb. 6, 1838 |
| JOHN MACNAUGHT | Apr. 7, 1815 | Aberdeen | Feb. 6, 1838 |
| JAS. LYNCH O'CONNER | Nov. 24, 1820 | Aberdeen | May 1, 1838 |
| JNO. T. INGLEBY | May 28, 1838 | Heidelberg | Nov. 6, 1838 |
| ROB. GEO. HOLLAND | June 12, 1838 | Erlangen | Nov. 6, 1838 |
| JNO. WARD DOWSLEY | Feb. 11, 1826 | St Andrews | Nov. 6, 1838 |
| JOHN MILLER | June 24, 1805 | Edinburgh | Feb. 5, 1839 |

## List of Fellows.

| Names of Fellows. | Dates of their Diplomas. | Places where they received their Degrees. | Dates of their admission as Fellows. |
|---|---|---|---|
| ANDREW HENDERSON | Aug. 1, 1823 | Edinburgh | Feb. 5, 1839 |
| J. STEVENSON BUSHNAN | May 14, 1836 | Heidelberg | Feb. 5, 1839 |
| RALPH F. AINSWORTH | Mar. 13, 1836 | Berlin | Feb. 5, 1839 |
| JAMES STARK | July 12, 1833 | Edinburgh | May 7, 1839 |
| THOMAS RADFORD | Apr. 4, 1839 | Heidelberg | Aug. 6, 1839 |
| KEITH IMRAY | June 28, 1836 | Pisa | Feb. 4, 1840 |
| JAMES ANDREW | July 2, 1839 | Cambridge | May 5, 1840 |
| ROB. BOWES MALCOLM | July 12, 1831 | Edinburgh | Aug. 4, 1840 |
| GEORGE LUND | Aug. 1, 1837 | Edinburgh | Aug. 4, 1840 |
| EVAN P. CAMERON | ... | ... | Aug. 4, 1840 |
| THOMAS R. COLLEDGE | Dec. 16, 1839 | Aberdeen | Aug. 4, 1840 |
| ALEXANDER WOOD | Aug. 1, 1839 | Edinburgh | Nov. 3, 1840 |
| JOHN WILLET | May 5, 1840 | St Andrews | Nov. 3, 1840 |
| Sir JNO. ROSE CORMACK | Aug. 1, 1837 | Edinburgh | Feb. 2, 1841 |
| GEORGE HULL | June 6, 1825 | St Andrews | Feb. 2, 1841 |
| HENRY HAWKINS | March 16, 1838 | Erlangen | Aug. 3, 1841 |
| HENRY LONSDALE | Aug. 1, 1838 | Edinburgh | Aug. 3, 1841 |
| JNO. HUGHES BENNETT | Aug. 1, 1837 | Edinburgh | Sept. 30, 1842 |
| DONALD MACFARLANE | Aug. 1, 1836 | Edinburgh | Nov. 1, 1842 |
| WILLIAM ROBERTSON | Aug. 1, 1839 | Edinburgh | Feb. 7, 1843 |
| AN. HALLIDAY DOUGLAS | Aug. 1, 1840 | Edinburgh | Feb. 7, 1843 |
| JOHN G. MACDONALD BURT | Nov. 9, 1836 | Giessen | May 2, 1843 |
| WILLIAM HALL RYOTT | Jan. 10, 1842 | Erlangen | May 2, 1843 |
| WILLIAM MACLEOD | May 2, 1843 | St Andrews | Aug. 1, 1843 |
| ALEXANDER JACKSON | Aug. 1, 1838 | Edinburgh | Nov. 7, 1843 |
| THEODORE F. WOOD | Aug. 1, 1843 | Edinburgh | Nov. 7, 1843 |
| JOHN BEEVOR | Aug. 3, 1841 | St Andrews | Feb. 6, 1844 |
| WILLIAM HUTCHESON | Aug. 1, 1838 | Edinburgh | Feb. 6, 1844 |
| W. M. ADAMS | Aug. 9, 1843 | Giessen | Nov. 5, 1844 |
| JOHN SCOTT | Aug. 1, 1820 | Edinburgh | Feb. 4, 1845 |
| EDWARD GREENHOW | Sept. 24, 1835 | Erlangen | Feb. 4, 1845 |
| JOHN COLDSTREAM | Aug. 1, 1827 | Edinburgh | Feb. 4, 1845 |
| ARCHIBALD MAKELLAR | April 25, 1832 | Glasgow | Feb. 4, 1845 |
| ROBERT PATERSON | Aug. 1, 1836 | Edinburgh | Feb. 4, 1845 |
| GEORGE S. KEITH | Aug. 1, 1841 | Edinburgh | Feb. 4, 1845 |
| WILLIAM BOWIE | Sept. 12, 1812 | Edinburgh | May 6, 1845 |
| NEVILLE WOOD | Aug. 1, 1844 | Edinburgh | May 6, 1845 |
| ALEXANDER PEDDIE | Aug. 1, 1835 | Edinburgh | May 27, 1845 |
| BEN. NORTH ARNOLD | April 6, 1840 | Giessen | May 27, 1845 |
| THOMAS SMITH MACCALL | April 24, 1838 | St Andrews | May 27, 1845 |
| THOMAS HUGHES | Aug. 1, 1825 | Edinburgh | Aug. 5, 1845 |
| WILLIAM MACKINNON | Aug. 1, 1836 | Edinburgh | Aug. 5, 1845 |
| THOMAS HEAD | May 6, 1845 | St Andrews | Aug. 5, 1845 |
| WILLIAM SCOTT | May 6, 1845 | St Andrews | Aug. 5, 1845 |
| SAMUEL D. LEES | Aug. 1, 1837 | Edinburgh | Nov. 4, 1845 |
| ALEXANDER SMITH | Jan. 28, 1826 | Aberdeen | Nov. 4, 1845 |
| JOHN G. HARRISON | June 6, 1842 | Giessen | Nov. 4, 1845 |
| BENJAMIN ROBINSON | May 7, 1839 | St Andrews | Nov. 4, 1845 |

## List of Fellows.

| Names of Fellows. | Dates of their Diplomas. | Places where they received their Degrees. | Dates of their admission as Fellows. |
|---|---|---|---|
| CHARLES CHADWICK | Aug. 1, 1837 | Edinburgh | Nov. 20, 1845 |
| J. CALTHROP WILLIAMS | Aug. 2, 1824 | Edinburgh | Nov. 20, 1845 |
| ROBERT BRENT | July 1, 1845 | St Andrews | Aug. 4, 1846 |
| WILLIAM HENRY LOWE | Aug. 1, 1840 | Edinburgh | Nov. 4, 1846 |
| ALFRED CRABB | May 5, 1846 | St Andrews | Nov. 7, 1846 |
| JOHN FERGUSON | June 1, 1815 | Edinburgh | Feb. 2, 1847 |
| JOHN SCOTT | Aug. 1, 1819 | Edinburgh | Feb. 2, 1847 |
| JAMES BEGBIE | Aug. 2, 1821 | Edinburgh | Feb. 2, 1847 |
| JOHN TAYLOR | July 12, 1830 | Edinburgh | Feb. 2, 1847 |
| THOMAS GRAHAM WEIR | Aug. 1, 1835 | Edinburgh | Feb. 2, 1847 |
| THOMAS STRETHILL WRIGHT | Aug. 1, 1845 | Edinburgh | May 4, 1847 |
| JOHN BROWN | July 12, 1833 | Edinburgh | Aug. 3, 1847 |
| EDWARD MACKAY | Sept. 25, 1844 | Giessen | Nov. 2, 1847 |
| NATH. AYLAN TRAVIS | Aug. 1, 1825 | Edinburgh | Dec. 2, 1847 |
| DAVID MACLAGAN | Sept. 12, 1805 | Edinburgh | Feb. 1, 1848 |
| FRED. BELL HUNT | May 6, 1845 | St Andrews | Feb. 1, 1848 |
| JAMES YORK | Dec. 15, 1832 | Erlangen | May 1, 1848 |
| JOHN CHARLES HALL | June 27, 1840 | Erlangen | May 1, 1848 |
| CHAS. RADCLYFFE HALL | Feb. 16, 1848 | Erlangen | Aug. 1, 1848 |
| EDWARD WATERS | Aug. 2, 1847 | Edinburgh | Aug. 1, 1848 |
| ALEXANDER KEILLER | Aug. 4, 1835 | St Andrews | April 5, 1849 |
| C. LOCKT. ROBERTSON | May 5, 1845 | St Andrews | May 1, 1849 |
| THOS. HILL PATTISON | July 12, 1831 | Edinburgh | Nov. 6, 1849 |
| JNO. YOUNG MYRTLE | July 12, 1833 | Edinburgh | Nov. 6, 1849 |
| SAMUEL SOMERVILLE | Aug. 1, 1836 | Edinburgh | Nov. 6, 1849 |
| WILLIAM CUMMING | Aug. 6, 1839 | St Andrews | Nov. 6, 1849 |
| FORBES BENJ. WINSLOW | April 13, 1849 | Aberdeen | Feb. 5, 1850 |
| WM. TENNANT GAIRDNER | Aug. 1, 1845 | Edinburgh | May 7, 1850 |
| WM. CHARLES WOOD | May 5, 1846 | St Andrews | May 7, 1850 |
| ALEX. A. RENTON | Aug. 1, 1849 | Edinburgh | Feb. 4, 1851 |
| JAMES MATT. DUNCAN | Oct. 16, 1846 | Aberdeen | May 6, 1851 |
| PETER NIDDRIE | April 29, 1835 | Glasgow | Dec. 4, 1851 |
| J. WARBURTON BEGBIE | Aug. 2, 1847 | Edinburgh | Feb. 3, 1852 |
| AWLY P. BARRON | Dec. 31, 1851 | St Andrews | May 4, 1852 |
| THOS. ALEX. WISE | Aug. 2, 1824 | Edinburgh | Aug. 3, 1852 |
| DANIEL RUTHERFORD HALDANE | Aug. 1, 1848 | Edinburgh | Aug. 3, 1852 |
| THOMAS T. WINGETT | Aug. 4, 1846 | St Andrews | May 3, 1853 |
| W. R. SANDERS | Aug. 1, 1849 | Edinburgh | May 3, 1853 |
| HENRY C. GURNEY | July 2, 1845 | Pisa | Nov. 1, 1853 |
| ALEXR. ZIEGLER | May 6, 1845 | St Andrews | Nov. 1, 1853 |
| JOHN SCOTT | Aug. 1, 1836 | Edinburgh | Feb. 7, 1854 |
| JOHN H. WALKER | Oct. 1853 | Aberdeen | March 2, 1854 |
| COURTLAND S. SHAW | Oct. 1853 | Aberdeen | May 2, 1854 |
| CHARLES WILSON | Aug. 1, 1827 | Edinburgh | Feb. 6, 1855 |
| JAMES ALLAN | Aug. 1, 1838 | Edinburgh | Feb. 6, 1855 |
| THOMAS GIBSON | April 25, 1827 | Glasgow | May 1, 1855 |
| WILLIAM J. MARTIN | April 14, 1855 | St Andrews | May 15, 1855 |
| THOMAS PRITCHARD | April 24, 1844 | Glasgow | July 10, 1855 |

## List of Fellows.

| Names of Fellows. | Dates of their Diplomas. | Places where they received their Degrees. | Dates of their admission as Fellows. |
|---|---|---|---|
| JOHN S. STEEL | April 7, 1854 | Aberdeen | Dec. 5, 1855 |
| THOMAS LAYCOCK | July 19, 1839 | Göttingen | Feb. 5, 1856 |
| GEORGE SAMPSON | Aug. 3, 1855 | Aberdeen | Aug. 5, 1856 |
| FREDERICK COLLINS | Aug. 6, 1851 | Aberdeen | Aug. 5, 1856 |
| WILLIAM E. TAYLOR | May 6, 1845 | St Andrews | Nov. 4, 1856 |
| WILLIAM KINGSLEY | July 1, 1845 | St Andrews | Feb. 3, 1857 |
| ARCHD. W. P. PINKERTON | Aug. 1, 1850 | Edinburgh | Aug. 4, 1857 |
| JOSEPH MARCUS JOSEPH | April 28, 1852 | Glasgow | Aug. 4, 1857 |
| CHARLES COATES | Oct. 1856 | Aberdeen | Aug. 4, 1857 |
| FREDERICK JOHN BIRD | May 4, 1841 | St Andrews | Feb. 2, 1858 |
| JAMES GEO. ATKINSON | Aug. 2, 1841 | Edinburgh | Feb. 9, 1858 |
| JAMES GAMMELL STEWART | Aug. 1, 1846 | Edinburgh | Feb. 9, 1858 |
| DONALD C. CAMPBELL | April 24, 1844 | Glasgow | May 4, 1858 |
| WILLIAM FINLAY | May 6, 1845 | St Andrews | May 18, 1858 |
| JOSEPH SEATON | May 6, 1845 | St Andrews | May 18, 1858 |
| T. HARRINGTON TUKE | Aug. 2, 1849 | St Andrews | Aug. 26, 1858 |
| GEORGE ALTHAM | Sept. 27, 1842 | Paris | Aug. 26, 1858 |
| GEORGE HARLEY | July 30, 1850 | Edinburgh | Aug. 26, 1858 |
| W. OVEREND PRIESTLEY | Aug. 1, 1853 | Edinburgh | Aug. 26, 1858 |
| JOHN MAULE SUTTON | Nov. 1, 1853 | St Andrews | Aug. 26, 1858 |
| JOHN SHAND | Aug. 1, 1844 | Edinburgh | Nov. 23, 1858 |
| KEATS ROBINSON RISK | Oct. 24, 1851 | Aberdeen | Nov. 23, 1858 |
| JAMES JOSEPH CREGEEN | Oct. 21, 1853 | St Andrews | Nov. 23, 1858 |
| JOHN HAYBALL PAUL | May 6, 1854 | St Andrews | Nov. 23, 1858 |
| THOS. BEATH CHRISTIE | May 6, 1854 | St Andrews | Nov. 23, 1858 |
| ROBERT CROSS | Aug. 1, 1854 | Edinburgh | Nov. 23, 1858 |
| HENRY KINGSLEY | Oct. 18, 1854 | Aberdeen | Nov. 23, 1858 |
| JOHN COCKER | Jan. 2, 1845 | Erlangen | Dec. 2, 1858 |
| THOS. HAYES JACKSON | Sept. 30, 1854 | Erlangen | Dec. 2, 1858 |
| A. M'NAMEE WALKER | Nov. 7, 1856 | Giessen | Dec. 2, 1858 |
| WILLIAM HELPS | May 6, 1854 | St Andrews | Dec. 28, 1858 |
| JOHN GODFREY | May 6, 1854 | St Andrews | Dec. 29, 1858 |
| W. FRED. HUTCHIESON RAMSAY | Aug. 2, 1848 | Glasgow | May 3, 1859 |
| J. DRUMMOND M'GAVIN | April 24, 1844 | Glasgow | May 3, 1859 |
| JAMES HOPE WATSON | Jan. 8, 1840 | Jena | Aug. 2, 1859 |
| G. MATHIESON OGILVIE | May 5, 1840 | St Andrews | Oct. 18, 1859 |
| JOHN CHALLICE | April 12, 1850 | Aberdeen | Feb. 28, 1860 |
| ROBERT BOWMAN | Aug. 1, 1852 | Edinburgh | Dec. 21, 1860 |
| GEORGE WILLIAM BALFOUR | May 6, 1845 | St Andrews | Aug. 6, 1861 |
| JAMES STRUTHERS | Aug. 1, 1848 | Edinburgh | Aug. 6, 1861 |
| ROBERT PEEL RITCHIE | Aug. 1, 1856 | Edinburgh | Aug. 6, 1861 |
| THOMAS GRAINGER STEWART | Aug. 1, 1858 | Edinburgh | Aug. 6, 1861 |
| WILLIAM ZIEGLER | Aug. 1, 1849 | Edinburgh | Nov. 5, 1861 |
| THOMAS JOHN GRAHAM | April 24, 1828 | Glasgow | Nov. 19, 1861 |
| DAVID CHRISTISON | Aug. 1, 1851 | Edinburgh | May 6, 1862 |
| LEWIS QUIER BOWERBANK | Aug. 1, 1836 | Edinburgh | Aug. 5, 1862 |
| R. EDMUND SCORESBY-JACKSON | Aug. 1, 1857 | Edinburgh | Aug. 5, 1862 |
| A. DOUGLAS MACLAGAN | Aug. 1, 1833 | Edinburgh | May 3, 1864 |

## List of Fellows.

### Admitted under Charter, dated 31st October 1861.

| Name of Fellows. | Qualifications. | Dates of admission as Members. | Dates of admission as Fellows. |
|---|---|---|---|
| REGINALD READ | L R.C.P. Ed., 1859 | Feb. 3, 1863 | Feb. 7, 1865 |
| JOHN LINTON | M.D. Edin., 1861 | Feb. 2, 1864 | May 2, 1865 |
| RICHARD FERNANDEZ FREEBORN | L.R.C.P. Ed., 1859 | Feb. 3, 1863 | Aug. 1, 1865 |
| CHARLES ROBINSON | L.R.C.P. Ed., 1860 | Nov. 3, 1863 | Aug. 1, 1865 |
| JOHN ALEXANDER SMITH | M.D. Edin., 1840 | Aug. 2, 1864 | Nov. 7, 1865 |
| ALEXANDER R. SIMPSON | M.D. Edin., 1856 | Aug. 2, 1864 | Nov. 7, 1865 |
| ALEXANDER CRUM BROWN | M.D. Edin., 1861 | Aug. 2, 1864 | Nov. 7, 1865 |
| ANDREW SMART | M.D. Edin., 1862 | Aug. 2, 1864 | Nov. 7, 1865 |
| CLAUD MUIRHEAD | M D. Edin., 1862 | Aug. 2, 1864 | Nov. 7, 1865 |
| JAMES RUTHERFORD | M.D. Edin., 1863 | Aug. 1, 1865 | Aug. 7, 1866 |
| ROBERT CRAIG MACLAGAN | M.D. Edin., 1860 | May 2, 1865 | Nov. 6, 1866 |
| ANDREW DAVIDSON | L.R.C.P. Ed., 1862 | Feb. 7, 1865 | Nov. 6, 1866 |
| WILLIAM ROSS | M.D. Glas, 1830 | Aug. 2, 1864 | Feb. 5, 1867 |
| JOHN GEORGE SINCLAIR COGHILL | M.D. Edin., 1857 | Feb. 7, 1865 | May 7, 1867 |
| WILLIAM HENRY BRACE | L.R.C.P. Ed., 1860 | May 1, 1865 | Aug. 6, 1867 |
| DAVID JAMES BRAKENRIDGE | M D. Edin., 1863 | May 1, 1866 | Aug. 6, 1867 |
| ALLEN DALZELL | M.D. Edin., 1853 | Nov. 6, 1866 | Nov. 5, 1867 |
| THOMAS HARDIE | M.D. Edin., 1858 | Aug. 1, 1865 | Feb. 4, 1868 |
| JOHN STEWARD | L.R.C.P. Ed , 1859 | Feb. 7, 1865 | Nov. 3, 1868 |
| THOMAS ALEX. GOLDIE BALFOUR | M.D. Edin., 1851 | Aug. 6, 1867 | Feb. 2, 1869 |
| GRIFFITH RICHARD JENKINS | L.R.C.P. Ed., 1867 | Feb. 4, 1868 | May 4, 1869 |
| ANGUS MACDONALD | M.D. Edin , 1864 | May 5, 1868 | May 4, 1869 |
| THOMAS RICHARD FRASER | M.D. Edin., 1862 | May 5, 1863 | Aug. 3, 1869 |
| JOHN MILLAR | M D Edin., 1863 | May 7, 1867 | Aug. 3, 1869 |
| WILLIAM JAMES HUNT | L.R.C.P. Ed., 1859 | Nov. 3, 1868 | Nov. 2, 1869 |
| JOHN WYLLIE | M.D. Edin., 1865 | May 4, 1869 | May 3, 1870 |
| JAMES ANDREW | M.D. Edin., 1866 | May 4, 1869 | May 3, 1870 |
| CHARLES GAGE BROWN | M.D. St And. 1851 | Nov. 5, 1867 | Aug. 2, 1870 |
| THOMAS COSSAR | M.D. Edin., 1841 | Aug. 3, 1869 | Nov. 1, 1870 |
| WILLIAM GORDON | M.D. Edin., 1862 | Nov. 2, 1869 | Nov. 1, 1870 |
| ROBERT JAMES WILSON | L.R.C.P. Ed., 1859 | Nov. 3, 1868 | Feb. 7, 1871 |
| WILLIAM WATSON CAMPBELL | M D. Edin., 1862 | May 1, 1866 | Feb 7, 1871 |
| JOHN BATTY TUKE | M.D. Edin., 1856 | Aug 2, 1870 | Nov. 7, 1871 |
| FRANCIS WALTER MOINET | M.D. Edin., 1867 | Feb 7, 1871 | May 7, 1872 |
| JAMES MURRAY FOSTER | L.R.C.P. Ed., 1865 | May 2, 1871 | Aug. 6, 1872 |
| HENRY WILLIAM HAIGH | L.R.C.P. Ed., 1869 | Aug 1, 1871 | Aug. 6, 1872 |
| JOHN GRAY M'KENDRICK | M.D Aberd., 1864 | May 2, 1871 | Aug. 6, 1872 |
| MORRISON WATSON | M.D. Edin., 1867 | May 2, 1871 | Aug. 6, 1872 |
| ARTHUR GAMGEE | M.D. Edin., 1862 | Feb. 7, 1871 | Nov. 5, 1872 |
| FRANCIS KENNEDY DICKSON | L.R.C.P. Ed., 1864 | May 7, 1872 | May 6, 1873 |
| THOMAS STRETCH DOWSE | M.D. Aberd., 1868 | May 7, 1872 | May 6, 1873 |
| JAMES CUMMING | M D. Edin., 1871 | Feb. 6, 1872 | Aug. 5, 1873 |
| JAMES BELL PETTIGREW | M.D. Edin., 1861 | Aug. 6, 1872 | Aug. 13, 1873 |
| THOMAS SMITH CLOUSTON | M.D. Edin., 1851 | Nov. 5, 1872 | Nov. 4, 1873 |

## List of Fellows.

| Name of Fellows. | Qualifications. | Dates of admission as Members. | Dates of admission as Fellows. |
|---|---|---|---|
| SAMUEL CARTRIGHT REED . . . | M.D. St And. 1862 | Feb. 4, 1873 | May 5, 1874 |
| ALEXANDER JAMES SINCLAIR . | M.D. Edin., 1872 | Feb. 4, 1873 | May 5, 1874 |
| PETER ALEXANDER YOUNG . . | M.D. Edin., 1870 | May 6, 1873 | May 5, 1874 |
| JOHN JANET KIRK DUNCANSON | M.D. Edin., 1871 | May 6, 1873 | May 5, 1874 |
| JOSEPH DOUGALL . . . . | M.D. Edin., 1872 | Nov. 4, 1873 | Nov. 3, 1874 |
| JAMES CARMICHAEL . . . . | M.D. Edin., 1864 | Feb. 3, 1874 | Feb. 2, 1875 |
| JOHN RICHARD CARMICHAEL . | L.R.C.P. Ed., | May 7, 1872 | May 4, 1875 |
| FRANCIS BOYNTON LEE . . . | L.R.C.P. Ed., 1869 | Feb. 3, 1874 | May 4, 1875 |
| JAMES ORMISTON AFFLECK . . | M.D. Edin., 1869 | May 5, 1874 | May 4, 1875 |
| THOMAS CHAMBERS . . . . | L.R.C.P. Ed., 1860 | Nov. 7, 1871 | Aug. 3, 1875 |
| WALTER ALFRED SATCHELL . | L.R.C.P. Ed., 1873 | Nov. 3, 1874 | May 2, 1876 |
| JOSEPH JOHN BROWN . . . | M.B. Edin., 1871 | Feb. 2, 1875 | May 2, 1876 |
| JOHN PLAYFAIR . . . . . | M.B. Edin., 1872 | Feb. 2, 1875 | May 2, 1876 |
| JOHN SIBBALD . . . . . | M.D. Edin., 1854 | Feb. 6, 1872 | Aug. 1, 1876 |
| HERBERT TIBBETS . . . . | L.R.C.P. Ld., 1865 | May 5, 1874 | Aug. 1, 1876 |
| CHARLES EDWARD UNDERHILL . | M.B. Camb., 1870 | Aug. 3, 1875 | Aug. 1, 1876 |
| JOHN PARKIN . . . . . | L.R.C.P. Ed., 1859 | Nov. 2, 1875 | Nov. 7, 1876 |
| KEITH NORMAN MACDONALD . | L.R.C.P. Ld., 1863 | Aug. 3, 1875 | Nov. 7, 1876 |
| THOMAS ANDERSON . . . . | M.B. Edin., 1871 | Aug. 4, 1874 | Nov. 7, 1876 |
| ALEXANDER BALLANTYNE . . | M.D. Edin., 1860 | Feb. 1, 1876 | Feb. 6, 1877 |
| ALEXANDER MONTGOMERIE BELL . | M.D. Edin., 1863 | Aug. 7, 1866 | May 1, 1877 |
| JOHN CONNEL . . . . . | M.D. Edin., 1873 | Feb. 1, 1876 | May 1, 1877 |
| DAVID HOPE WATSON . . . | L.R.C.P. Ed., 1859 | May 2, 1876 | May 1, 1877 |
| WILLIAM RUTHERFORD . . . | M.D. Edin., 1863 | May 2, 1876 | May 1, 1877 |
| WILLIAM ALLAN JAMIESON . . | M.B. Edin., 1865 | May 2, 1876 | May 1, 1877 |
| CHARLES FRERE WEBB . . . | L.R.C.P. Ed., 1871 | May 5, 1874 | Aug. 7, 1877 |
| HENRY MORRIS . . . . . | L.R.C.P. Ld., 1875 | Aug. 1, 1876 | Nov. 6, 1877 |
| EDWARD CHARLES ROBSON . . | L.R.C.P. Ed., | May 4, 1875 | Dec. 14, 1877 |
| WILLIAM JOHN HENRY LUSH . | L.R.C.P. Ed., 1873 | Feb. 1, 1876 | Dec 14, 1877 |
| ALEXANDER JAMES . . . . | M.D. Edin., 1877 | Aug. 7, 1877 | Dec. 14, 1877 |
| CHARLES FIELD GOLDSBRO'. . | L.R.C.P. Ed., 1860 | Feb. 1, 1876 | Feb. 5, 1878 |
| JAMES FOULIS . . . . . | M.B. Edin., 1872 | Feb. 6, 1877 | May 7, 1878 |
| THOMAS INGLIS . . . . . | L.R.C.P. Ed., 1874 | Feb. 6, 1877 | May 7, 1878 |
| HENRY JECKELL KENDRICK VINES . | L.R.C.P. Ed., 1869 | May 1, 1877 | May 7, 1878 |
| GEORGE HERON AITCHISON . | M.B. Edin., 1872 | May 1, 1877 | May 7, 1878 |
| FREDERICK EMMET BECK . . | L.R.C.P. Ed., 1867 | Feb. 6, 1877 | Aug. 6, 1878 |
| WILLIAM MILSTED HARMER. . | L.R C.P. Ed., 1864 | Feb. 7, 1865 | Nov. 5, 1878 |
| WILLIAM STEWART . . . . | L.R C P. Ed., 1864 | May 1, 1877 | Nov. 5, 1878 |
| REGINALD LOUIS VERLEY . . | L.R.C.P. Ed., 1872 | Aug. 4, 1874 | Feb. 4, 1879 |
| THOMAS RUTHERFORD RONALDSON | M.D. Edin., 1874 | Aug. 7, 1877 | Feb. 4, 1879 |
| HERVEY EUSTACE ASTLES . . | L.R C.P. Ed., 1867 | Nov. 6, 1877 | May 6, 1879 |
| HENRY MACDONALD CHURCH . | M.D. Edin., 1874 | Feb 5, 1878 | May 6, 1879 |
| JOHN BROWN BUIST . . . . | M.D. Edin., 1871 | May 7, 1878 | May 6, 1879 |
| THOMAS OUTTERSON WOOD . | L R C P. Ed., 1868 | Nov. 3, 1874 | Aug. 5, 1879 |
| PETER M'BRIDE . . . . . | M B. Edin., 1876 | May 6, 1879 | May 4, 1880 |
| RICHARD JAMES MAITLAND COFFIN | L.R.C.P. Ed., 1874 | Aug. 4, 1874 | Aug. 3, 1880 |
| BRYOM BRAMWELL . . . . | M.D. Edin., 1877 | Aug. 5, 1879 | Aug. 3, 1880 |

## List of Fellows.

| Name of Fellows. | Qualifications. | Dates of admission as Members. | Dates of admission as Fellows. |
|---|---|---|---|
| GEORGE ALEXANDER GIBSON | M.B. Edin., 1876 | Aug. 5, 1879 | Aug. 3, 1880 |
| JAMES MURDOCH BROWN | M.D. Edin., 1874 | May 1, 1877 | Nov. 2, 1880 |
| JOHN HALLIDAY CROOM | M.B. Edin., 1868 | Feb. 5, 1878 | Nov. 2, 1880 |
| DAVID BERRY HART | M.D. Edin., 1877 | May 6, 1879 | Nov. 2, 1880 |
| WALTER WEIR | M.B. Edin., 1878 | Aug. 5, 1879 | Nov. 2, 1880 |
| JAMES ALEXANDER RUSSELL | M.B. Edin., 1868 | Nov. 4, 1879 | Nov. 2, 1880 |
| THOMAS WHITEHEAD REID | L.R.C.P. Ld., 1875 | Feb. 3, 1880 | May 3, 1881 |
| STEPHEN COULL MACKENZIE | M.D. Edin., 1864 | Aug. 2, 1870 | Aug 2, 1881 |
| CHARLES ORTON | L.R.C.P. Ed., 1865 | May 6, 1879 | Aug. 2, 1881 |
| ALFRED BOYLE THOMPSON | L.R.C.P. Ed., 1860 | Feb. 3, 1880 | Aug. 2, 1881 |
| ALFRED JAMES AITKINSON | L.R.C.P. Ed., 1871 | May 4, 1875 | Nov. 1, 1881 |
| CHARLES BROWNE | L.R.C.P. Ed., 1874 | May 4, 1680 | Nov. 1, 1881 |
| JAMES ALLAN GRAY | M.B. Edin., 1876 | Aug 3, 1880 | Nov. 1, 1881 |
| WILLIAM SMITH GREENFIELD | M D. Lond., 1874 | Aug. 2, 1881 | Nov. 1, 1881 |
| PETER YOUNG | M.D. Edin., 1857 | Feb. 1, 1881 | Feb. 7, 1882 |
| JOHN JAMES GRAHAM BROWN | M.D. Edin., 1878 | May 3, 1881 | May 2, 1882 |
| MARCUS HENRY ALLEN | L.R.C.P. Ed., 1871 | May 6, 1873 | Aug 1, 1882 |
| GEORGE FOWLER | L.R.C.P. Ed., 1864 | Aug. 5, 1873 | Aug. 1, 1882 |

C

# LIST

OF

## Honorary Members of the College

FROM ITS ERECTION, WITH THE DATES OF THEIR ADMISSION

N.B.—*The Record is wanting from December 1652 to the year 1694.*

| Names of Honorary Members. | Dates of their admission. | Names of Honorary Members. | Dates of their admission. |
|---|---|---|---|
| EARL OF MARCHMONT | May 15, 1696 | M. DE SENAC | Nov. 4, 1760 |
| LORD WHITEHILL | ... | JOHN EARL OF BUTE | Nov. 3, 1761 |
| LORD ANSTRUTHER | Nov. 6, 1699 | DR JAMES MOUNSEY | Nov. 2, 1762 |
| DR DAVID GREGORY | Aug. 22, 1705 | COUNT CARBURY | Nov. 5, 1765 |
| DR ROBERT GRAY | Oct. 4, 1705 | SIR CHARLES LINNEUS | Nov. 3, 1772 |
| SIR HANS SLOAN | Oct. 4, 1705 | BARON ALBERT VON HALLER | Nov. 3, 1772 |
| EARL OF WEMYSS | Dec. 13, 1705 | | |
| LAIRD OF POSSO | Nov. 14, 1706 | HENRY DUKE OF BUCCLEUCH | Dec. 2, 1773 |
| EARL OF LEVEN | April 22, 1707 | | |
| EARL OF ERROLL | June 3, 1707 | DR H. GAUBIUS | Dec. 2, 1773 |
| EARL OF GLASGOW | ... | DR JAS. FLINT, *ex officio* | May 3, 1774 |
| LORD PRESTONHALL | June 18, 1707 | DR ANT. STÖRCK | Nov. 5, 1776 |
| LORD MINTO | ... | DR J. G. ZIMMERMAN | Dec. 5, 1782 |
| DR JOHN ARBUTHNOT | Dec. 12, 1707 | DR J. M. DE LASSONE | Dec. 5, 1782 |
| DR ALEX. RUSSELL | Feb. 12, 1712 | SIR JOS. BANKS, BART. | ... |
| DR WILL. COCKBURN | May 5, 1724 | DR JOHN ROGERSON | ... |
| DR GEORGE CHEYNE | ... | GEORGE DUKE OF MONTAGUE | Dec. 17, 1782 |
| DR JAMES CAMBBELL | May 2, 1727 | | |
| DR WILL. FULLERTON | Nov. 5, 1728 | DR P. CAMPER | ... |
| DR GEORGE MARTIN | Aug. 5, 1740 | DR FEL. VICQ. D'AZYR | Feb. 2, 1790 |
| DR DAVID BALFOUR | Feb. 7, 1744 | DR JO. AND. MURRAY | ... |
| DR JOHN JOHNSTON | ... | DR AUG. GOT. RICHTER | Dec. 1, 1791 |
| DR THOMAS SIMPSON | Feb. 7, 1744 | | |
| DR RICHARD MEAD | May 7, 1745 | DR JO. GOT. WALTER | ... |
| DR JAS. M'KENZIE | Oct. 2, 1755 | SIR GEO. BAKER, BART. | Mar. 27, 1792 |
| DR JOHN HUXHAM | Oct. 2, 1755 | COUNT RUMFORD | Nov. 4, 1800 |
| DR G. VAN SWIETEN | Nov. 4, 1755 | DR EDWARD JENNER | May 20, 1806 |
| ARCH. DUKE OF ARGYLE | Nov. 30, 1758 | DR MATTHEW BAILLIE | Nov. 13, 1809 |

# LIST

## OF

## Presidents of the College

FROM ITS ERECTION.

---

Sir ARCHIBALD STEVENSONE, elected President 8th December 1681, and continued till 1684.

Sir ROBERT SIBBALD elected 4th December 1684.

---

*From 1684 to 1693 the Record is wanting.*

| Names of Presidents. | Dates of their Election. | Names of Presidents. | Dates of their Election. |
|---|---|---|---|
| Sir ARCH. STEVENSONE | Nov. 30, 1693 | Dr JOHN GARDINER | Dec. 5, 1782 |
| Dr ROBERT TROTTER | Dec. 6, 1694 | Dr JOHN HOPE | Dec. 2, 1784 |
| Sir THOMAS BURNET | Dec. 3, 1696 | Dr JAMES HAY | Nov. 30, 1786 |
| Dr MAT. SINCLARE | Dec. 1, 1698 | Dr JOSEPH BLACK | Dec. 4, 1788 |
| Dr ROBERT TROTTER | Dec. 5, 1700 | Dr AND. DUNCAN | Dec. 2, 1790 |
| Dr ALEX. DUNDAS | Dec. 3, 1702 | Dr JAMES HAMILTON | Dec. 6, 1792 |
| Dr JAMES HALKET | Nov. 30, 1704 | Dr NATHANIEL SPENS | Dec. 4, 1794 |
| Dr WILLIAM ECCLES | Dec. 5, 1706 | Dr D. RUTHERFORD | Dec. 1, 1796 |
| Dr MAT. SINCLARE | Dec. 2, 1708 | Dr JAMES GREGORY | Dec. 6, 1798 |
| Dr WILL STEWART | Dec. 6, 1716 | Dr WILL. WRIGHT | Dec. 3, 1801 |
| Dr JAMES FORREST | Dec. 3, 1719 | Dr THOMAS SPENS | Dec. 1, 1803 |
| Dr JOHN DRUMMOND | Dec. 6, 1722 | Dr CHARLES STUART | Dec. 4, 1806 |
| Dr FRANCIS PRINGLE | Nov. 30, 1727 | Dr JAMES HOME | Nov. 30, 1809 |
| Dr JOHN RIDDELL | Dec. 2, 1731 | Dr J. HAMILTON, Jun | Dec. 3, 1812 |
| Dr ROBERT LOWIS | Dec. 4, 1735 | Dr THOS. CHAS. HOPE | Nov. 30, 1815 |
| Dr JOHN CLERK | Dec. 4, 1740 | Dr JAMES BUCHAN | Dec. 2, 1819 |
| Dr WILL. COCHRAN | Dec. 6, 1744 | Dr AND DUNCAN, Jun. | Dec. 5, 1822 |
| Dr W. PORTERFIELD | Dec. 1, 1748 | Dr AND. DUNCAN, Sen. | Dec. 4, 1824 |
| Dr JO. RUTHERFORD | Nov. 30, 1752 | Dr ALEX. MONRO | Dec. 1, 1825 |
| Sir ALEX. DICK | Dec. 2, 1756 | Sir ALEX. MORISON | Dec. 6, 1827 |
| Dr ROBERT WHYTT | Dec 1, 1763 | Dr J. H. DAVIDSON | Dec. 3, 1829 |
| Sir S. THRIEPLAND | Dec. 4, 1766 | Dr J. MACWHIRTER | Dec. 1, 1831 |
| Dr JOHN BOSWELL | Dec. 6, 1770 | Dr J. H. DAVIDSON | Dec. 5, 1833 |
| Dr COLIN DRUMMOND | Dec. 3, 1772 | Dr JOHN THOMSON | Dec. 4, 1834 |
| Dr WILLIAM CULLEN | Aug. 3, 1773 | Dr W. P. ALISON | Dec. 1, 1836 |
| Dr FRANCIS HOME | Nov. 30, 1775 | Sir R. CHRISTISON | Dec. 6, 1838 |
| Dr GREGORY GRANT | Dec. 4, 1777 | Dr R. GRAHAM | Dec. 3, 1840 |
| Dr ALEX. MONRO | Dec. 3, 1779 | Dr R. RENTON | Dec. 1, 1842 |

## List of Presidents.

| Names of Presidents. | Dates of their Election. | Names of Presidents. | Dates of their Election. |
|---|---|---|---|
| Dr W BEILBY | Dec 5, 1844 | Dr JOHN G. M. BURT | Dec. 3, 1863 |
| Sir R. CHRISTISON | Dec. 3, 1846 | Dr JOHN SMITH | Nov. 30, 1865 |
| Dr W SELLER | Nov. 30, 1848 | Dr JOHN MOIR | Dec. 5, 1867 |
| Sir J. Y SIMPSON | Dec. 5, 1850 | Dr A H. DOUGLAS | Dec. 2, 1869 |
| Dr THOS. S. TRAILL | Dec. 2, 1852 | Dr R. PATERSON | Nov. 30, 1871 |
| Dr JAMES BEGBIE | Nov. 30, 1854 | Dr W. H. LOWE | Dec. 4, 1873 |
| Dr DAVID MACLAGAN | Dec. 4, 1856 | Dr ALEX. KEILLER | Dec. 2, 1875 |
| Dr ALEXANDER WOOD | Dec. 2, 1858 | Dr ALEX. PEDDIE | Dec. 6, 1877 |
| Dr DAVID CRAIGIE | Dec. 5, 1861 | Dr D. R. HALDANE | Dec. 4, 1879 |

# Historical Sketch

OF THE

# ROYAL COLLEGE OF PHYSICIANS.

THE attempt to incorporate the Practitioners of Medicine in Scotland for the purpose of raising the standard both of the character and acquirements of Physicians, originated in 1617. King James I. of England, to whom an application for that purpose was made, received it favourably, and issued an order to the Parliament for the establishment of a College of Physicians in Edinburgh. This order is still extant. After reciting the evils which the community had suffered from the intrusion of irregular practitioners, it directs the Parliament to form a College of Physicians, appoints seven persons to examine those who proposed to practice Medicine, and makes it illegal for any person to exercise the art and science of Physic within Edinburgh and the neighbourhood, without the Diploma of the College.

*Early attempts at formation of a College.*

*Order of James I.*

His Majesty also farther suggests that warrant should be given to the College to appoint yearly three of its number to visit the Apothecaries' shops in the burgh, to examine the state of the drugs exposed for sale, and to destroy such as might be found corrupt or insufficient.

*How frustrated.*

Dissensions, chiefly of a religious kind, had the effect of preventing the wishes of the King from being carried out.

*Renewal of attempt, 1630.*

In 1630 the attempt was renewed, and King Charles I. referred the matter to his Privy Council; but, owing chiefly to the unsettled state of public affairs, nothing more was done in his reign.

*Patent by Cromwell, 1656.*

The matter was warmly taken up by Cromwell during his Protectorate; and a patent, still extant, was made out in 1656, instituting a College of Physicians of Scotland, "who shall have power and authority to oversie, rule, and order, what may concerne the right administratioune of Physike to the people of Scotland in all pairts and places of the said nation, with power to them to censure and punish all persons who shall presume to practise, exercise, or profess Physike, or give medicines, or ordaine Physicall Praescriptiones in any pairt or place of Scotland, being not members of the said Colledge, or not being approved and licensed by the said Praesident and Colledge under their Common Seal." Farther, in this patent of Incorporation, it was proposed to give to the said President and College the power to practise the Art of Surgery: "forasmuch as the Science of Physick doth comprehend, include, and containe in it the knowledge of Chirurgery, being a special part of the same and member thereof." By it, also, the power of examining and licensing Apothecaries, and of visiting their shops, was to be conferred on the proposed College; and, lastly, the College was to be entitled to receive from the magistrates of the several cities and burghs, and the sheriffs of the respective counties, "such dead bodies of malefactors executed as they shall desyre, for making of dissection and anatomie for the use of the Colledge."

The extensive powers thus proposed to be conferred naturally created jealousies among the other public Medical bodies, and before the various conferences for the adjustment of these differences were ended, the death of the Protector put a stop for a time to the whole scheme.  *Frustrated by other Medical Bodies and death of Cromwell.*

Eventually, though not without great opposition on the part of the Surgeons, the Universities, the Municipal Corporation, and even the Bishops and Archbishops, a Charter of Incorporation was obtained from Charles II., and the Great Seal was appended to this charter on St Andrew's Day, 1681.  *Charter of 1681.*

This Charter commenced by laying down the necessity which existed for ascertaining that those who design to practise any profession should be examined as to their capacity for doing so, and stated that from the absence of any regulation of this kind regarding Medicine, great confusion had arisen, and many very ill qualified persons exercised the healing art. It then proceeded to institute the College of Physicians as a great and powerful means of correcting this abuse. It ordained that the College should consist of certain individuals who were named, and of all others who might be chosen by them as Colleagues and Fellows of their Society, within the city of Edinburgh, its Suburbs and Liberties: so that they and their successors should be united and conjoined into one Body, Community, and College, in all time coming. The Charter further provided for the election of a Council, President, and other Office-Bearers, and conferred on the College the power to enact Laws for its due government  *Summary of contents of Charter of 1681.*

and welfare, and for promoting the Science and regulating the practice of Medicine within the City of Edinburgh and Leith, their Suburbs and Liberties.

*Summary of contents of Charter of 1681.*

It prevented, under certain penalties, any one from practising Medicine within the jurisdiction of the College who had not obtained its Licence or Diploma.

It conferred on the College the power, under certain regulations, of calling before it and fining unlicensed practitioners, and also of punishing all Physicians, Doctors of Medicine, Licentiates, and Fellows practising within their jurisdiction, who might violate any of the Laws of the College.

The College was farther invested by the Charter with power to examine, along with a magistrate and chemist, the Medicines kept in the Apothecaries' shops, and to destroy such as were not found to be of good quality.

The Charter also prevented the Magistrates from allowing any one to open an Apothecary's shop until he had, by an examination, satisfied the President and Censors of the College that he had a competent knowledge of drugs.

The Charter farther provided, that no Fellow of the College should be cited as a juror on any assize in town or country, or be called out to watch or ward, or on any pretext whatever be withdrawn from his patients.

*Several Powers conferred by Charter of 1681 not exercised.*

The College continued to discharge its functions under this Charter for many years, although it eventually abandoned in practice the exclusive rights conferred on it, and ceased to exercise any inspection over the shops of the Apothecaries. In fact, the changes of social position necessarily caused many of the provisions to fall into abeyance.

*Reasons why a new Charter was desirable.*

The College had not been insensible to the advantages that would accrue to it from obtaining a new

## Historical Sketch.

Charter, more especially that it might thereby free itself from the obligation laid on it of admitting to its licence all Scottish University Graduates without examination and without a ballot, and also that it might get rid of the clause prohibiting it from being connected with a Medical School, and farther, that it might obtain the power of expelling unworthy Members.

The subject of a new Charter had repeatedly been considered by the College, but was always delayed, in the hope of the settlement of the long-vexed question of Medical Reform.

In 1843, when the late Sir James Graham, then Home Secretary, had all but succeeded in carrying a Bill for Medical Reform, the College instructed the late Mr Richard Mackenzie, W.S., to prepare the draft of a new Charter, which, after revision by the College, was finally adjusted in 1845 by Mr Drinkwater Bethune, the Government official, but the abandonment by Sir James Graham of his Bill caused it to be laid aside.

On the 9th of May 1854 the long-forgotten draft was referred to the Medical Reform Committee for its consideration and amendment, and the Committee reported on the 1st May following. Fresh discussions on Medical Reform again interrupted procedure regarding it, and it was not until the Medical Act had received the Royal Assent in July 1858 that the subject was again resumed. On the 21st of September of that year the Committee of the College on Medical Reform presented to the College a very full and exhaustive report on the manner in which the College would probably be affected by the Medical Act (21 and 22 Victoriæ, 1858).

This Report fairly brought before the College the propriety of obtaining a new Charter, as it was authorised to do by clause 49 of the Act. The objects to be kept in view were stated in this Report to be, *First*, To give the College a wider designation, The Royal College of Physicians of Scotland ; *Second*, To get rid, if possible, of the restrictive clauses in the existing Charter ; *Third*, To introduce an order of Members ; *Fourth*, To obtain power to examine, should the College choose it, all applicants for the Licence, whether University Graduates or not ; *Fifth*, Should the power of examination not be given or exercised, to have power to apply the ballot ; *Sixth*, To have the undoubted power of the suspension and expulsion of unworthy Members vested in the College.

On the 21st of December the College took this part of the Report into consideration, and resolved to apply for a new Charter. At several meetings thereafter (28th and 29th December 1858, and 18th February and 1st March 1859) the College discussed the draft of the proposed Charter. Considerable difference of opinion was manifested, chiefly in regard to whether the College should admit to its Fellowship other than University Graduates, and whether the College should get rid of the restriction which prevented it from erecting a Medical School. Both these questions were at length decided in the affirmative. The College also introduced a clause to enable it to hold property in its corporate name. Between the period when the new Charter was agreed to by the College and the date of its being granted, the College, on a Report by the Council, agreed to retain the name of Royal College of Physicians of Edinburgh, in preference to that of Royal College of Physicians of Scotland, which the Medical Act authorised her Majesty to bestow. This resolution was come to on the 5th February 1861, and the new

## Historical Sketch.

Charter was obtained, dated the 16th August, and sealed and registered on the 31st October 1861.

This Charter sets out by reciting the petition of the College for the grant of a new Charter. Clause first constitutes the President, the Vice-President, the Members of Council of the College and their successors, and the other existing Fellows and all who shall hereafter be admitted Fellows or Members, a body corporate, with all the rights and privileges usually appertaining to corporate bodies.

Clause 2 gives to the College, as constituted by the new Charter, the right to all property of whatever description, which belonged to it under the former Charter.

Clause 3 constitutes the existing Fellows the first Fellows of the College as newly incorporated.

Clause 4 gives power to admit new Fellows and Members under such regulations, and on payment of such fees as the College may from time to time ordain.

Clause 5 gives power to grant Licenses.

Clause 6 gives power to the College, with consent of three-fourths of the Members present, to censure, suspend, or depose any Fellow, Member, or Licentiate of the College who has obtained admission by false pretences, or violated any of the bye-laws.

Clauses 7 to 10 regulate the Ordinary and Extraordinary Meetings of the College.

Clauses 11 to 17 regulate the appointment of the Office-Bearers.

Clause 18 arranges for the management of the property and affairs of the College.

Clause 19 secures the validity of the acts of the College, notwithstanding any informality in the election of the President or of any Councillor.

Clause 20 gives to the College power to make

bye-laws for promoting the Science of Medicine, for duly ordering the practice of the same, and for the good government, order, and direction of the College.

Clause 21 continues the existing bye-laws in force until new ones are passed.

Clause 22 gives to the new College, its Fellows, Members, and Licentiates, all the powers enjoyed by the existing College, and those connected with it.

Among the other changes effected by this Charter was the power given to the College to elect its President directly, and not through the intervention of the Council; and the abolition of the offices of Censors and Fiscal, the duties of which having long been in abeyance, the names were now finally relinquished.

Returning to the history of the College after the first Charter (1681) had been obtained, we find it enter with great zeal on the discharge of the duties committed to it.

The publication of a Pharmacopœia was undertaken, and arrangements were made for regular attendance on the sick poor.

The loss of the earlier Minutes renders it very difficult to ascertain where the meetings of the College were at first held. Dr Beilby, in his Address at the opening of the present Hall, stated that the first and several subsequent meetings were held in the house of Sir Robert Sibbald, but there seems no sufficient authority for this; and it is evident that what follows in Dr Beilby's narrative, is founded on his having misread the name of Dr (afterwards Sir Archibald) Stevenson for that of Johnstone.

The cause of the door being locked in the faces of the President and Fellows by Dr Stevenson, which Dr Beilby was unable to explain, is rendered sufficiently clear by a reference to the disputes in which Dr Pitcairn

## Historical Sketch.

and Sir Archibald Stevenson were so conspicuous, all mention of which were, however, erased from the Minutes by authority of the College.*

On the 24th May 1697 the Treasurer was authorised to pay £3, 10s. to Mr William Livingstone for a year's rent of the room in which the College met, and half a dollar to the maid. *Mr Livingstone's House*

On 17th April 1698, the College resolved unanimously to buy a house of its own, and two days afterwards a Committee was authorised to offer £75 for the house of Mr Livingstone, where the College then met. This offer probably proved insufficient, as the College continued to meet in apartments rented for the purpose, until, in 1704, it acquired the house and grounds of Sir James Mackenzie, in Fountain Close in the High Street. *First Hall in Fountain Close, 1704.*

This property, purchased for £194, 8s. 10d., immediately adjoined that of the Marquis of Tweeddale; and when, seven years subsequently, the College acquired the land belonging to Bailie Jeffrey (price £127, 14s. 11d.), which lay between their first purchase and the then fashionable Cowgate, the extent of the gardens and shrubbery were the envy of the neighbouring Peers, to several of whom the privilege of walking in them was, at their request, permitted as a favour. *Situation of first Hall.* *Its extensive Gardens*

It throws a curious light on the manners and customs of our ancestors, and on the absence of what are now considered indispensable arrangements for personal comfort in every private dwelling, to find that the College converted certain ruinous buildings which bordered on the Cowgate, into a pavilion-shaped cold bath, which was open to the inhabitants generally, at a charge for each ablution of 12 shillings Scots and *Public Bath.*

---

\* Paterson's Abstract of the Minutes.

one penny to the servant. But those who subscribed one guinea annually might resort to it as often as they pleased.

At first a Committee of the Physicians appears to have attended to receive the fees and superintend the ablutions; but this having been found inconvenient, the President was allowed to let the bath on lease.

In 1714 the bath was let to Alexander Murray and John Russell of Bradshaw, W.S. The speculation does not seem to have been a successful one, as they and several successive tenants were continually craving for an abatement of the rent, while the bath was as continually requiring repair.

*New Hall erected in the Garden at Fountain Close, 1722. Proved insufficient.*

In 1722 a new Hall was erected in the garden, the necessary funds having been borrowed from Robert Marshall, merchant in Edinburgh.

"Notwithstanding," says Dr Beilby, "all the sums that had been expended in the erection of a *new* building, and in the repair of the *old*, the former seems to have been slight and insufficient, and the latter was in so dilapidated a condition, that in 1760 it was resolved to build a new Hall upon the premises then held by the College, and a plan was obtained and approved, the execution of which was to cost £800, a sum that was declared to be within the means of the College; but before commencing the work, it was determined to submit the design to the judgment of Mr Robert Adam, the King's Architect, who, after inspecting it, gave it as his opinion that it was unsuitable, and quite unworthy of the Body for which it was intended;—and, with great liberality, Mr Adam gave, spontaneously and gratuitously, a plan of his own, the execution of which was estimated to cost between £5000 and £6000, exclusive of the statues, busts, and bas-reliefs, which he recom-

*An entirely new building resolved on*

*Plan of Mr Adam.*

mended as appropriate and almost necessary. This plan, after being handed about and admired, was laid aside as unsuitable to the finances of the College.

"At length, however, such was the state of the College buildings, that the books were suffering great injury, and it became absolutely necessary to remove them without further delay. Application was made to the Managers of the Royal Infirmary for permission to deposit the Library in a spare apartment of that building, and also for liberty to hold the meetings of the College in the Managers' Board-room. These requests were readily granted, and the privilege was continued to the College for fifteen years. The Library had now become so extensive, that it was insured for £600.

<small>*Royal Infirmary affords a Temporary Asylum.*</small>

"By this time a design had been formed, and some progress had already been made, towards laying out a New Town in the northern vicinity of the city. To this situation the eyes of the College were turned, as being greatly preferable to that which it had hitherto occupied. A petition was presented to the Town Council for a site, and the negotiation was nearly concluded for the lot of ground on which the Register Office now stands, for which the College was to have paid a feu-duty of £8 sterling per annum; but Mr Adam, the architect who was employed by Government to give a design for the Register Office, perceiving how peculiarly desirable that situation was for the noble building he intended to erect, had influence enough to prevent the consummation of the transaction, and to secure that site for himself.

<small>*New Town Site sought there.*</small>

<small>*Site of present Register Office all but obtained.*</small>

"The Town Council then agreed to give a site just where the Scott Monument has been erected; but this was deemed by the College ineligible. A choice of two sites was next offered,—the one in George Square and the other in George Street, the latter of

<small>*Site of one of Scott Monument offered and rejected.*</small>

*Site of present Commercial Bank to be selected*

*Debt entailed on College by new Hall.*

*Proposal to sell new Hall.*

which was finally fixed upon, being destined to receive in succession two buildings of more pure and refined taste, perhaps, than any others in the city.

"The premises in Fountain Close were sold in 1770 for £800, being intended for the site of an Episcopal chapel. The Hall in George Street was not commenced till 1776, when the foundation-stone was laid by Dr Cullen, the President. About £4800 were expended upon it. This, notwithstanding all the efforts made to procure subscriptions, plunged the College into debt to the extent of nearly £1000, for which sum the Hall was immediately mortgaged. Some of the Fellows were now so despondent about the state of the treasury, that before ever the College had entered upon the occupation of it, a proposal was brought forward to sell the building. A negotiation was entered into with a party for the purpose of its being converted into Assembly Rooms,—the stream of fashion having by this time begun to flow towards the New Town, and some of the Lady Directresses of the Edinburgh 'Almack's' having become dissatisfied with their dingy apartments in Bell's Wynd. The sale was agreed upon, the price to be paid was £3750; missives had actually passed, and the College, by a majority, had sanctioned the act of their Committee, when, most fortunately, it was saved from the indelible disgrace into which it was plunging, by some of the Lady Directresses changing their minds, when they began to reflect on the remoteness of the locality from the residences of the greater part of them, and the danger they might incur of an overturn of their chairs while crossing the newly erected bridge over the North Loch, in the dark and stormy nights of winter. This 'second thought' came fortunately in aid of a resolution, which had already been formed by some of the objecting Fellows, to endeavour to get the transaction rescinded by an appeal to the Courts of Law. In the end the College relinquished all intention of selling the building, and all trace of the proceedings relative to it was removed from the Minutes. It was now resolved to take possession of the New Hall without farther delay, submitting to whatever inconvenience might be sustained from the yet unfinished state of the interior. The College assembled in it for the first time on the 7th of August 1781, just one hundred years after being first incorporated."

During the subsequent removal of that building, after being disposed of by the College under circumstances to be immediately narrated, the foundation-stone was discovered in May 1845. A well-cut inscription on this interesting relic sets forth that it was laid on the 27th November 1775 by the President, Dr Cullen. Inclosed in the stone, a bottle was found, containing, 1st, A Parchment Roll, on which are beautifully inscribed the names of the Fellows of the College at the time ; 2d, Several British Coins of date 1771 ; 3d, A Silver Medal, representing on the one side the future College, surmounted by the words, 'ARTI SALUTIFERAE SACRUM, at its base a serpent entwined round a club ; on the other side—

<pre>
            AEDES
        COLL. REG. MED.
            EDINB.
         HIC POSITAE
      XXVII NOV. A.D. MDCCLXXV
         CURANTE PRAESIDE
         GULIELMO CULLEN
            ARCHITECTO
           JAC. CRAIG.
</pre>

*Margin notes: Hall in George Street. Foundation Stone. Laid by Professor Cullen. Inscription on Medal.*

4th, Another Silver Medal, having the arms of the City of Edinburgh on the one side, and on the other an inscription, bearing that this memorial had been presented to Mr Craig, Architect, by the Council of the City of Edinburgh, in compliment to his professional talents, in the year 1767. It is as follows :—

JACOBO CRAIG
ARCHITECTO
PROPTER OPTIMAM
EDINBURGI NOVI
ICHONOGRAPHIAM
D . D
SENATUS
EDINBURGENUS
M'DCCLXVII.

These interesting relics of an age gone by are now in the possession of the College.

The same poverty which had prevented the College from availing itself of the plans of Adam, and which had caused it to desire to part with its New Hall in George Street, even before it had entered on its occupation, still pressed heavily on it. Having at that time no funded capital, it was entirely dependent on the entrance fees paid by Fellows, a fluctuating and inadequate source of income. Besides, beautiful as the George Street Hall was in its outward proportions, its internal arrangements were not so convenient as might have been desired, and it is therefore not to be wondered at that when the College found that its site was coveted by a wealthy banking corporation, its poverty and not its will consented ; and in 1843 the George Street Hall was sold to the Commercial Bank for £20,000,—a sum which it was hoped would suffice to build a more commodious, if less imposing, Hall, and leave a surplus to secure a certain annual income.

Although the transaction was obviously an advantageous one for the College, it was not without some difficulty that many of the Fellows made up their minds to part with a building of which they were justly proud. *[Reluctantly parted with...]*

On the 8th of August 1844, the foundation-stone of the present Hall was laid by the President, Dr Renton, in presence of the Fellows of the College, and various representative persons. As is customary on such occasions, a bottle containing various memorials was deposited in the stone. In this instance these were—1st, A copy of the last edition of the Edinburgh Pharmacopœia, containing a list of the Fellows of the College; 2d, A work regarding the private affairs of the College, printed several years previously; 3d, An Edinburgh Almanac for the current year; 4th, Several British Coins of the day; and lastly, A silver plate with an inscription in Latin suitable to the occasion. *[Hall in Queen Street, 1844]*

During the erection of the Hall the College rented for its use a private house, No. 121 George Street, from which, in 1846, it removed to its present building. *[Temporary sojourn in George Street]*

Ample as the accommodation of the Hall appeared to be at the date of its erection, the rapid additions to the Library, and the great increase in the number of Fellows, consequent on a reduction of the entry money, and other changes, soon rendered some extension necessary. *[Insufficiency of Hall for accommodation of Library]*

After long and anxious deliberation, and much delicate negotiation, the Trustees, on the recommendation of the Council, agreed to purchase from the Trustees of the late Dr Reid, formerly Principal of the

Edinburgh Institution for Languages and Mathematics, the building in which the business of that Seminary was conducted.

The purchase was made in 1865 for £6000, but the house was then under a lease to the successors of the late Dr Reid, which did not expire until May 1867. This house, No. 8 Queen Street, which immediately adjoins the Hall on the east, had been built and occupied as his residence by Baron Orde, and considerably exceeds in size the other houses in the street.

Considerable difference of opinion existed as to how the new purchase could be made most available for the extension of the present Hall. Mr Bryce, as instructed by the Council, prepared a plan for a New Library, to extend along the back of the existing Hall and of the new purchase, and this plan was laid before the College. It was ultimately, however, agreed to carry out so far the design of Mr Hamilton, the architect who planned the original building, and double the size of the existing Hall, by extending it backwards, at the same time completely altering the character of the roof according to suggestions made by Mr Bryce, with the view of increasing the light and improving the acoustic properties of the Hall. Additional accommodation for books was provided by arranging round the new Hall dwarf bookcases, which would, it was supposed, contain all the additions which the Library was likely to acquire for some years to come. At the same time a spacious building was erected at the back of the adjoining house, which was leased for a term of years to the proprietors of the Institution, with a view to its ultimately affording additional accommodation for the Library. But so rapidly has the accumulation of books gone on, that it has already been found necessary to connect this building with the Hall, and convert it into a Library capable of containing about twenty-five thousand volumes.

It will be apparent to every one who has perused the preceding pages, that the College of Physicians was not, until very recently, a wealthy body; and yet, as has been observed by Dr Poole (Appendix to Report on Licensing), "it has throughout its career manifested a conduct that would do honour to a rich community." . . . "It appears to have existed purely for the welfare of society."  *Beneficent Deeds of the College.*

On the 7th February 1738 the Members were recommended to encourage the design of founding an Orphan Hospital. In return for the assistance afforded, the President of the College is still *ex officio* a Governor of that Institution.  *Assists the Orphan Hospital.*

On the 3d of May 1744, £50 was unanimously voted by the College to aid in the erection of an Episcopal Chapel on the site formerly possessed by the College in Fountain Close. This building is now in possession of, and used by, the Roman Catholics.  *Subscribes to erection of Episcopal Chapel in the Cowgate.*

On the 20th March 1775, fifty guineas was subscribed towards the erection of the High School, which was afterwards converted into part of the Surgical Hospital; and this at a time when extraordinary efforts were being made to raise the necessary funds to erect the Hall in George Street.  *Subscribes to erection of High School.*

On the 13th November 1789, the sum of £150 was subscribed to assist in the erection of the University of Edinburgh; when, rather more than eighty years later, a scheme was set on foot for extending the scientific and educational buildings of the University, the College, on the 6th May 1873, subscribed a sum of one thousand guineas in aid of it.  *Subscribes to erection of New University Buildings.*

On examining the Minutes it will be found that many of our oldest Charitable Institutions were indebted to the College for pecuniary aid—as the Blind Asylum, the Lunatic Asylum (more than once), and the Charity Workhouse.

In 1874 one hundred guineas was voted in aid of the Building Fund of the Royal Maternity Hospital, and in 1875 fifty guineas in aid of the Livingstone Medical Missionary Memorial Dispensary.

In 1871 fifty guineas was subscribed to the local fund for defraying the expenses of the reception of the British Association in Edinburgh; and in 1881 fifty pounds was voted towards defraying the expenses of the International Medical Congress which met in London.

Among other liberal donations may also be chronicled one to the National Monument in 1822, of fifty guineas; and the same day (30th August) one of a like amount for a statue to commemorate the visit of George IV. to his Scottish metropolis; one of fifty pounds for a statue of Dr Jenner at Gloucester, 4th November 1823; one to the Scottish National Memorial of the late Prince Consort of twenty-five guineas on the 20th June 1862; and one of twenty-five guineas to the fund for erecting a statue to Dr David Livingstone, African explorer. On 5th May 1863, one hundred pounds was voted by the College to assist in repairing the tomb of the late Dr Cullen, in Kirknewton burial ground. On the 24th February 1880, the sum of one hundred guineas was voted in aid of the fund for the Restoration of the Cathedral Church of St Giles.

Two hundred pounds was voted for the relief of the poor in the famine of 1796. On the 24th December 1878 a sum of two hundred and fifty guineas was voted in aid of the fund for the relief of the sufferers by the failure of the City of Glasgow Bank.

On the 15th February 1796, £200 was voted towards the defence of the country "in the present exigency of public affairs." In return for this liberality, the Government, judging of the capabilities of the College more by its generosity than by its actual income, imposed a Stamp Duty upon the Diplomas of its Licentiates and Fellows —the former of which was only, after repeated application, removed in 1859; while the latter still exists.

*National Defence Fund.*

*Tax imposed upon Fellows and Licentiates.*

Besides these donations to public objects, the College seem to have been not unmindful of the claims of their own Fellows, and occasional contributions to the widows of deceased Fellows are recorded in the Minutes. Sundry donations to the College also seem to have called forth a pecuniary return, as when, on two occasions (August 4, 1713; January 11, 1715) the College voted a guinea to Mr Alexander Bruce for a book he had presented to the Library; and, in 1717, two guineas to Mr Gordon, surgeon, Aberdeen, "for a great excrescence he had removed from a person's cheek, and complimented the College therewith." In 1696 the College presented to the University a Boat, honestly avowing that it was because there was no place in the College to keep it, to which is appended the additional reason, that the University had already the oars and the skirt of the barbarous man that was in it. This boat seems to have come into possession of the College as one of Sir A. Balfour's curiosities.

*Donations to Widows of Fellows.*

*Curious presents, and their acknowledgment.*

To the College of Physicians also the public are indebted for the origin of some of our best Medical Charities. A care for the sick poor manifested itself at a very early period of its history; for we find that at the third meeting of the College (10th February 1682), two Physicians were appointed to serve the poor of the City and Suburbs.

*Care for the Sick Poor.*

These appointments continued to be regularly made; but the Physicians, "in serving the poor," found all their efforts often unavailing, from the want of suitable accommodation, diet, and nursing, and accordingly about 1725, the plan of an Infirmary was suggested by the College to several well-disposed persons; and the scheme having been favourably received by them, a public meeting was called to make the proposal known. Thereafter, on the 1st February 1726, we find the following Minute:—

"The President represented to the College that according to their desire, he and several of the members had set on foot a subscription for erecting and maintaining an Infirmary or Hospital for the sick poor, and had pretty good success; and recommended to all the Members of the College to use their best endeavours to procure more subscriptions for accomplishing so good and charitable a work."

On 1st August 1727, the College bound itself by a Minute, "that one or more of their number shall attend the said Hospital faithfully and freely, without any prospect of reward or salary, until the Stock of the said Hospital shall be so increased that it can afford a reasonable allowance for one or two physicians."

On 7th November 1727, appears a Minute, "That the Members of the College had sett this charitable work on foot;" and on the 7th May 1728, the College memorialized, and sent a deputation to the General Assembly of the Church of Scotland, calling the attention of that Reverend Body to the value of the proposed charity.

On the 5th August 1729, the Minutes of the College show that a temporary Hospital was established by it, in which the sick poor were attended by its Fellows.

*Marginalia:* Erection of Infirmary first suggested by College. — Minute regarding commencement of Infirmary, February 1726. — Undertake the Medical charge of the Infirmary gratuitously. — College memorializes General Assembly on behalf of Infirmary. — College open a temporary Infirmary.

## Historical Sketch.

It will be seen from the History of the Royal Infirmary, published by authority (1778), that as soon as £2000 had been subscribed, "The College of Physicians called the Contributors together; at this meeting a Committee was appointed, who prepared a report regarding the management, which was submitted to a second meeting, when twenty Managers were elected." The Infirmary was incorporated by Royal Charter, by a deed dated 27th August 1736. By this Charter five of the Managers *at least*, must be Fellows of the College.

At a meeting of the College, 7th February 1738, a letter was read from the Managers of the Royal Infirmary, stating that it had been resolved for the future that none but Fellows of the College were to act as Physicians to that charity.

1st August 1738.—The College attended as a body at the laying of the foundation-stone of the Royal Infirmary; and the next day voted thirty guineas to the funds, to be raised by voluntary contribution.

On the 2d November 1742, the College ordained that each Fellow should, on admission to the College, pay twenty shillings to the Infirmary.

2d February 1785.—The College voted fifty guineas to the funds of the Royal Infirmary.

On the 2d February 1819 the College, on account of the expense incident to the prevalence of fever, voted fifty guineas to the Infirmary, and ten guineas to the Society for preventing contagious fever.

It having been decided to remove the Royal Infirmary to a new site, and a public subscription having been instituted to provide the necessary funds, the College, on the 18th February 1868, voted the sum of £1000 in aid of this object.

On the 3d May 1879, the College agreed to contribute a sufficient sum (£630) to furnish two Medical Wards in the New Royal Infirmary.

On the 29th October 1879, the College attended as a Body at the inauguration of the New Royal Infirmary.

There are many other Minutes showing the close and intimate relationship subsisting between the College and the Infirmary; and it should be known to all the Fellows that the College can insist that none but its Fellows shall act as Physicians to the noble institution which it was mainly instrumental in founding.

The Royal Edinburgh Asylum for the Insane at Morningside, also owes its origin to the enlightened liberality of the College of Physicians. On the 2d of August 1791, a Committee reported to a Quarterly Meeting of the College on the propriety of placing the Private Asylums under regulation, and also of erecting a Public Asylum near Edinburgh, similar to one at York. This Report pointed out that if Trustees in whom the public had confidence were appointed to manage the proposed Asylum, donations and bequests might be expected to come in. It farther suggested that the Trustees, to whom a sum of money had been left by the late Mr Watson to establish a Foundling Hospital, should be applied to, to give it to the proposed Lunatic Asylum, as being a charity of a less doubtful character. It also proposed the names of those who should be Trustees. This Report was unanimously adopted by the College, and was the first movement which led to the formation of the present magnificent establishment at Morningside.

The publication of a Pharmacopœia engaged much of the attention of the College, and it was issued in 1799; from that time the publication of successive editions enabled the College to keep pace with the progress of scientific discovery.

When, however, the Medical Act of 1858 conferred on the General Council of Medical Education and Registration the power of issuing a Pharmacopœia, which should be obligatory in all three divisions of the kingdom, the College, on the 1st of July 1862, gave its formal assent to the introduction into Parliament of a Bill, the effect of which was that the British Pharmacopœia, published by the General Medical Council, superseded in Scotland the Pharmacopœia published by the College of Physicians.

The College, restricted by its original Charter in many ways—prevented from connecting itself with any Medical School—compelled to receive, without examination and without ballot, the Graduates of all Scottish Universities, and having allowed any power of licensing which it had possessed to pass from it by desuetude, occupied a position of a very peculiar character among the Medical Bodies. Highly respectable and respected, containing among its Fellows the most eminent Physicians in Edinburgh, and the Medical Professors of the University, full of good works and charity, it never comprised any large proportion of those practising medicine in Edinburgh, or in Scotland, who usually joined the College of Surgeons.

This state of matters existed, notwithstanding the exclusive privileges which the Fellows of the College possessed, of being the only Physicians of the Infirmary, and of certain of the Dispensaries in the city. The unsatisfactory condition of such a state of matters, as bearing upon the real interest and due importance of the College pressed itself, at various times, on the attention of the Fellows.

Up to 1829 the College had issued a Licence to practise; but this was given, as the Charter required, to all University Graduates, without examination. It was conferred on no others; and on 1st November 1763, the Licentiateship was made a necessary stepping-stone to the Fellowship of the College. Finding, however, that by making each Fellow pass through the grade of Licentiate, the College compelled him to pay a double tax to Government, this regulation was abolished in 1829, and the Fellows being elected without passing through the inferior grade, the old order of Licentiates ceased to exist.

On two several occasions an elaborate Report was drawn up and printed, strongly recommending the College to admit another class of Licentiates, who should derive their Qualification to practise directly from the College; but, besides that, such a measure was of doubtful legality, influences were at work within the College which were sufficient to frustrate all efforts in that direction.

In the meantime, however, certain changes in the Extra-Academical School, particularly the working of a regulation, which required every Teacher of Medicine or Surgery to belong to, and subsequently to be examined as to his capabilities for teaching by a College of Physicians or Surgeons, were gradually introducing a new element into the College, and associating it with interests very different from those with which, in its earliest years, it had been inseparably connected.

It would be a tedious task to enumerate all the keen discussions to which the struggle between the party which had long been dominant in the Councils of the College, and that which was gradually springing up, gave rise; even the copious Minutes of the Meetings

## Historical Sketch. 43

held during the protracted contendings scarcely serve to record their extent; suffice it to say, that the passing of the Medical Act of 1858 inaugurated a new era in the history of the College. An elaborate Report on the manner in which the Act would affect the College was presented by the Council to the College on the 21st September 1859, in which it was argued, that the admission of Licentiates other than University Graduates was, in the altered state of the whole medical profession, absolutely essential for the credit of the profession, as well as for the very existence of the College. It will probably appear strange to those Fellows who have joined the College since 1860, and who hear read at each Quarterly Meeting the long list of Licentiates admitted by examination, that the proposal to examine and confer a Licence on gentlemen who had not previously obtained a University degree, was strenuously resisted, not only by Professors of the University, but by a large number of Fellows who had no direct connection with that Body, and that it was ultimately carried on the 5th of April 1859, only by the vote of one Fellow; and that there actually appears in the Minutes of the College (26th April 1859) a protest, signed by ten Fellows, against the Licence being conferred on any but University Graduates.

The College having, however, resolved to examine and admit to the profession, as Licentiates of their Body, gentlemen who had no other qualifications to practise, or who might wish to possess the Licence of the College in addition to qualifications already obtained, proceeded to consider a Report of the Council, suggesting the regulations under which the Licence should be conferred. As one of these regulations was unfortunate enough to provoke keen discussions in the College, as

*Report on Medical Act.*

*Recommends a new order of Licentiates*

*Proposal to Licen e other than University Graduates.*

*Strenuously resisted.*

*Carried by one vote. Protested against.*

*Resolution to license.*

well as hostile criticisms on its policy from without; and as the proceedings of the College in this respect have been, and still are, the subject of misrepresentation, it appears essential, even in this slight sketch of its history, to enter somewhat fully into an explanation of the motives which actuated the College in a matter which has been the subject of so much controversy.

With regard to the permanent regulations, the amount of study and of examination required of Candidates for the Licence has never been considered otherwise than sufficient, it was the exceptional admissions, during what was termed the Year of Grace, which excited all the clamour with which the College was assailed.

The College had been compelled, by its Charter of 1681, drawn up under the influence of the Scottish Universities, to admit all Graduates of these Bodies within its ranks without examination. There existed various Licensing Bodies, which required of their Licentiates an education and examination equal to that of any, and superior to that of some, of these Universities. The London College of Physicians had passed regulations extending for one year the privilege of becoming Licentiates of their Body to all Graduates or Licentiates of Universities in Great Britain, simply requiring of them the recommendation of three Fellows, and the test of the ballot. The Commissioners for the Improvement of the Scottish Universities had intimated that the Degrees of these Bodies were henceforth to be considered as Licences for general practice. Under these circumstances, it was strongly urged upon the Council of the College, that it would be a right and fitting thing to inaugurate the new era in Medical practice, by extending for a limited period, to men equally well educated and equally qualified to practise, the privilege long enjoyed by University Licentiates, of entering the Body without examination. This Act of Grace was intended for a large body of men of mature age, who, having begun life as Surgeons or Apothecaries, had established their position as good Practitioners, and were naturally anxious to be connected with a Body of higher position than a Trading Company.

Many young men did, undoubtedly, apply for admission, but, with few exceptions, they were told that they must undergo an examination, as the Regulations of the "Year of Grace" were only intended for Practitioners of mature age. The securities instituted by the College to prevent the conferring of the Licence on unsuitable persons were the following—

1. That the Candidate had passed the examination of one or more of the Licensing Boards.
2. That he must give up the sale of drugs, if he had previously dealt in them.
3. That he must produce certificates of his fitness to be a Licentiate of a College of Physicians from Hospital Physicians, or men of eminence in the profession.
4. That his claims for admission must be carefully scrutinised by the Council of the College.
5. That these claims must be subjected to a ballot in the College, a majority of two-thirds of those who voted, being essential to his admission.

These appeared to the College to be better tests of the fitness of men to be Licentiates of the College, than the subjecting them to an examination framed for Students fresh from their studies. They were in strict accordance with the principles of an *ad eundem* admission which almost every Licensing Body at that time permitted.

The boon thus offered was sought for with an eagerness which startled even those who had been most forward in urging it. In fact, it was its very success which provoked the attacks made upon it. Another circumstance, naturally calculated to excite jealousy was, that many of the Licentiates of the College, possessing no University Degree, at once proceeded to call themselves "Doctors of Medicine." Unjustifiable as this was, the Edinburgh College of Physicians was not chargeable with any blame in the matter; it had encouraged no such assumption of titles. The mistake, as far as it could be traced, seemed to have arisen from the old practice of the London College of Physicians to style all its Licentiates Doctors. That this is no mere surmise appears from the fact, that the then newly appointed Registrar under the Medical Act, who had long been Registrar to the London College of Physicians, at first gave the title of Doctor to the Licentiates of the Edinburgh College, in the receipt granted to them for their Registration-fee; and from the other fact, that as the agitation proceeded, the title of M.D., which had long stood after the names of many gentlemen in the Army and Navy Lists, who had no other claim to that title than that these gentlemen were Licentiates of the London College of Physicians, began rapidly to disappear from these Lists.

It may be, as indeed was afterwards admitted, that a privilege which, in the opinion of the College, might safely have been extended to gentlemen who had previously been examined and licensed in Medicine, ought not to have been offered to those who only held a Surgical Qualification, and who had undergone no examination in Medicine.

Probably those who proposed the scheme, at a time when the requirements of the various Licensing Bodies were not so well known as they now are, overlooked the fact, that there were Bodies Licensing for practice which did not examine in Medicine; certain it is that the mistake was no sooner pointed out than it was rectified, by the institution of an examination in Medicine alone, to be passed by those Candidates who had not already been subjected to that ordeal.

The jealousy and rancour which had been excited were not, however, to be easily appeased. The Medical Press still reiterated their charge against the College, of "Selling Licences" to practise. The London College of Physicians was induced to remonstrate with the Edinburgh College, which it did in the most courteous terms. A reply, equally courteous, was forwarded to it, pointing out the reasons which had induced the Edinburgh College to modify its terms of admission; and regulations subsequently passed by the London College would appear to show that in some important respects it had become converted to the views of the Edinburgh College. It indeed was the inventor of what was called a Year of Grace, during which it agreed to admit certain men to its Licence without farther examination. The Edinburgh College imitated its example; but, in consequence of the different state of Medical practice in Scotland, and its consequently different position, its admissions were on a wider scale. If the giving of Licences without examination be a crime, and if it is to be stigmatised as a Sale of Licences, both Colleges are reprehensible, as well as every other Examining Board which admitted *ad eundem* Licentiates, as most of them did at that period.

It would be difficult to prove that the Licentiates of the various Bodies who were admitted without examination to the Edinburgh College, were inferior in medical

knowledge and ability to practise their profession, to many Licentiates of Universities who were eligible for admission to the Licence, without examination.

The British Medical Association, a Body which contained in its ranks a large number of Fellows of the Royal College of Physicians of Edinburgh, and which, during its recent meeting in Edinburgh, had received the utmost hospitality and encouragement from the Edinburgh College, acting on the unwarrantable publication of a private letter, addressed by a Fellow of the Edinburgh College to one of its Members, without requesting, or even giving any opportunity for explanation from the College or any of its Fellows, passed a resolution condemnatory of its Regulations,—a piece of interference, on the part of a self-constituted body of a most reprehensible kind, and which had the effect of causing a number of its most distinguished Edinburgh Members to withdraw from its ranks. Ultimately, at a meeting of the Medical Council, Sir D. J. Corrigan, on the 8th of August 1859, moved, "That the General Medical Council is of opinion that any Degree or Licence obtained since the passing of the Medical Act, without regular examination by the University or College granting such degree or Licence, ought not to be placed on the *Register*, excepting *ad eundem* Degrees, or Degrees and Licences in Medicine or Surgery of any University in the United Kingdom, admitted to the Fellowships or Licentiateships of the several Colleges of Physicians and Surgeons." This motion was strenuously resisted. Dr Alexander Wood, the President of the Edinburgh College, and its Representative in the Medical Council, showed the real position of the question, and the unfair advantage which such a resolution would give to the Graduates and Licentiates of

## Historical Sketch. 49

Universities; after which the Medical Council adopted an amendment to Sir D. Corrigan's motion, proposed by Dr Wood, namely, "That the General Medical Council are of opinion that for the future no Licence or Degree should be given by any of the Bodies in Schedule (A) to the Medical Act, without examination."

Since the publication of this opinion no one has received a Licence without examination; but the examination is modified and restricted in the case of gentlemen already holding a Licence to practise. It may not be out of place to state here, that long before the passing of the Medical Act, it had become the conviction of the leading Fellows of the College, that it had been a highly impolitic proceeding on the part of the London College of Physicians to refuse the offer made to it by the Government, in the year 1815, to undertake the licensing of General Practitioners in England, as by so doing that important office was thrown into the hands of a trading Company of Apothecaries, and thereby the name of Apothecary, as that of a Medical Practitioner, was legalised, instead of one of the time-honoured names—Physician or Surgeon; that they were desirous of having the name of Apothecary, as applied to a Medical Practitioner, wiped out without delay; that, at the same time, they recognised the excellence of the Regulations acted on for a number of years by the Apothecaries' Company with regard to their curriculum and examinations, and therefore they felt themselves called on, as soon as it was in the power of the College, to offer to those gentlemen who had been compelled, for many years, to put up with the title of Apothecary, the opportunity of exchanging it for that of a Licentiate of a College of Physicians, provided they could produce testimonials of respectability and ability in the past conduct of their practice.

Such is a brief outline of this most critical part of the history of the College, with which it is incumbent on every Fellow to be acquainted, and regarding which explanations are often asked even at the present day.

But the College had still a serious difficulty to contend against in the shape of a tax of Fifteen Pounds imposed on every Licence which was issued. By the Medical Act all exclusive privileges enjoyed by certain Bodies had been swept away, and the Licentiates of any of the Bodies in Schedule (A) to the Medical Act had an equal right to practise Medicine and Surgery, or Medicine or Surgery, in any part of her Majesty's dominions. The Licentiates of Colleges of Physicians, and the Graduates of Universities, were alone subjected to a Stamp Duty, and this proved an important obstacle to any increase in their number. Various attempts had been made at various periods to obtain a remission of these duties, but without success.

On the 27th November 1858, Dr Alexander Wood, then President of the College, and its Representative in the Medical Council, moved that Body to memorialize the Lords of her Majesty's Treasury on the subject. This memorial was not prepared or transmitted till the 5th February 1859. No effect having been produced by it, Dr Wood endeavoured to organise a joint deputation from the three Royal Colleges of Physicians, to the Treasury, but without success. Ultimately, at the request of the Council, he proceeded to London, and on the 20th May 1859, he received the announcement that the Stamp Duty of Fifteen Pounds on the Diploma of Licentiates would be remitted. For his services on this occasion the President received a special vote of thanks from the College at its meeting on the 14th June 1859; and for his other invaluable services in placing the College on the advantageous footing which it had lately attained, it was unanimously resolved, in the following year, to present him with his portrait, painted by Sir John Watson Gordon.

*Acknowledgement of services of Dr Wood.*

Other difficulties still beset the College in regard to its new Licence. The English Poor Law Board, and the Army Medical Board, not being previously aware of its existence, refused to recognise it as a sufficient Medical Qualification. This led to a correspondence between the heads of these Bodies and the President of the College, and eventually Dr Wood, proceeding to London, succeeded in obtaining the recognition of the Licence of the College, which was thereafter regarded as a sufficient Medical Qualification.

*Recognition by Poor Law Board and Army Medical Board.*

In 1859 an important arrangement was made with the Royal College of Surgeons of Edinburgh and the Faculty of Physicians and Surgeons of Glasgow, both of these Bodies having the right to license in Surgery, by which the addition of the Licence in Medicine of the Royal College of Physicians of Edinburgh confers upon the holder the right to practise all branches of the profession in every part of her Majesty's dominions.

*Arrangement with College of Surgeons of Edinburgh, and Glasgow Faculty for "Double Qualification."*

This "Double Qualification" is eagerly sought after; and the College has thus been enabled, after long and arduous struggles, to exercise the licensing functions legitimately appertaining to such a Body; and while containing on its Roll of Fellows the names of the most distinguished Physicians in Scotland, to confer the right to practise Medicine on a numerous and increasing body of general Practitioners.

The terms on which this alliance was formed will be best understood from the following proposals

*Conditions of Double Qualification.*

submitted to the General Council of Medical Education and Registration, on the 6th of August 1859, and approved of by that Body on the 8th of the same month:—

"1. By Clause 19 of the Medical Act, 'any two or more of the Colleges and Bodies mentioned in Schedule (A) may, with the sanction and under the directions of the General Medical Council, unite or co-operate in conducting the Examinations for Qualifications to be registered under this Act.' Hence it is quite competent for a College of Physicians and a College of Surgeons to combine, in order, by a Joint Examination, to give a Double Qualification, embracing Medicine and Surgery.

"2. Co-operation between a College of Physicians and a College of Surgeons being legal, as stated above, the Colleges of Physicians and Surgeons of Edinburgh propose, with the sanction of the General Medical Council, to make an arrangement for the purpose of granting, by a series of Examinations, Preliminary and Professional, their respective Licences in Medicine and Surgery, so as to constitute a Double Qualification.

"3. It is proposed that the Preliminary Examination in Literature and Science, and also the Examinations on those professional subjects which are common to Medicine and Surgery, shall be conducted conjointly by a Board formed of Examiners in equal proportions from the two Colleges.

"4. It is proposed that the Examinations in *Medicine* shall be conducted exclusively by Examiners from the College of Physicians, and the Examinations in *Surgery* exclusively by Examiners from the College of Surgeons.

"5. It is proposed that the decision as to the competency of the Candidate in all the Branches except Medicine and Surgery, shall rest with the conjoined Board of Examiners from the two Colleges; but that the decision as to his competency in Medicine and in Surgery shall rest entirely, in the one case with the Examiners from the College of

Physicians, in the other case with the Examiners from the College of Surgeons.

"6. It is proposed that having passed through the final Examinations, the Candidate shall receive two separate Diplomas—one from each College—signed by the Office Bearers of each respectively, so that he may be enabled to produce them to the Registrar under the Medical Act, and to register two separate Qualifications—viz., L.R.C.P. Ed., and L.R.C S. Ed.

"7. The Colleges wish it to be clearly understood, that such co-operation is not to interfere in any degree with the right of each College to grant its Diploma separately, as heretofore, to those who may wish a Single Qualification, or with the right of each College to make similar arrangements with other Licensing Bodies, if deemed expedient, and if sanctioned by the Medical Council.

"8. For the purpose of carrying out the objects stated above, the Colleges have prepared a Series of Regulations, which they beg now to submit to the Medical Council for their consideration."

As already stated, the College obtained power by its Charter of 1861, to institute an order of Members who should be intermediate in rank between the Licentiates and the Fellows. No special privileges were conferred upon the Members; but a Law was passed to the effect that no one should be eligible for the Fellowship until he had been at least one year a Member of the College. At first the only qualifications for the Membership were, that the Candidate should be a Licentiate of a College of Physicians, or a Graduate of a British or Irish University; that he should have attained the age of twenty-four years; that he should produce satisfactory testimonials as to his social and professional status; and that a motion for his election should be carried by a majority of not less than three-fourths of the Fellows voting. Under these conditions a large and constantly increasing number of Members was admitted. In course of time however, the opinion began to gain ground among the Fellows, that these conditions of admission were unsatisfactory, and that it was desirable that an examination should be instituted, which all candidates for the Membership should be required to pass. The subject was brought before the College from time to time, but was delayed in the hope that some comprehensive measure of Medical Reform would be introduced by the Government. As years, however, passed, and no such measure was proposed, the subject was taken up seriously, and on the 24th February 1880 a Committee was appointed to consider the Laws relative to admission to the Membership and Fellowship of the College. After a good deal of discussion at several meetings of the College, the Report of the Committee was, on the 1st February 1881, approved of, and the Laws relative to admission were agreed to as they now stand. In conformity with these Laws, Candidates for the Membership are required, before they are balloted for, to pass an examination on Medicine and Therapeutics, as well as on one of the following subjects, to be selected by themselves—(*a*) Pathology and Morbid Anatomy; (*b*) Medical Jurisprudence and Public Health; (*c*) Midwifery and the Diseases of Women; (*d*) Psychological Medicine. Power, is however, given to the Council to exempt from examination Candidates over forty years of age who have been Registered Practitioners for not less than ten years, and who have been highly distinguished for their scientific or practical attainments. The immediate effect of this change in the conditions of admission has been to diminish very largely the number of Candidates.

*Marginalia:*
- Proposal to establish an Examination.
- Laws as to admission to Membership.
- In certain cases examination may be dispensed with.

## Historical Sketch. 55

The College, looking to the increasingly important position occupied by State Medicine, resolved, on the 29th December 1874, to establish a certificate of Qualification in that subject; and on the 4th May 1875, agreed to the Regulations under which it is now granted.

*Qualification in State Medicine.*

From the date of its Incorporation in 1681, the attention of the College appears to have been steadily directed to the formation of a Library. Sir Robert Sibbald, to whose exertions the College is mainly indebted for its Charter, was a large contributor to the Library. Two years after the Incorporation of the College a Librarian was appointed. The Library was, during the earlier years of its existence, enriched by donations from Fellows of the College, eminent Physicians, and individuals of distinction not even connected with the Medical Profession.

*Library.*

*How commenced.*

The following Chronological Notes as to the progress of the Library may be interesting, from the references made in them to many of the former Fellows to whom the College is indebted for valuable services in connection with it, which have helped to bring it to its present satisfactory condition.

*Notes as to progress of Library.*

In 1683 Dr Archibald Stevenson was elected Librarian, and Dr Pitcairne, Deputy-Librarian.

In 1696 a law was enacted, that every Intrant should contribute a book or books to the Library; and numerous donations of single books are noticed from time to time in the Minutes of several following years—one consequence of which was, that duplicates, and works unsuited to a Medical Library, began to accumulate, which were every now and then ordered to be sold, and new medical books to be purchased in their stead. In 1713 it was resolved that the Fellows should have

*Every Fellow to contribute a Book on entering, 1696.*

the option of buying such duplicates before they were put up to auction.

*Purchase of the Laird of Livingstone's Books.*

In 1705 a considerable addition was made to the Library by the purchase of the books of the deceased Laird of Livingstone for 300 merks Scots (about £16, 13s.). The first Library Committee seems to have been appointed at the end of that year; for the Minutes bear, that on December 13, Sir R. Sibbald, Drs Smelholm, Riddell, and Luitfoot, with the President, Censors, and Library-keeper, were appointed Curators and Overseers of the Library.

*Bequest of Books of Dr John Drummond.*

In 1741 the College came into possession of the library of a former President, Dr John Drummond, after his decease, by the Bequest of David Drummond, Advocate, his brother and heir. Two conditions were attached to the Bequest, namely, that these books should be kept in presses by themselves, and that none of them should be lent out unless the full value was deposited with the Keeper of the Library. The College formally accepted the conditions, and took measures to comply with them; but by the lapse of time, and by the repeated transferences of the Library, these conditions were unfortunately lost sight of, and can now no longer be fulfilled. It seems probable that this oversight is to be accounted for, in a great measure, by the sudden removal of the books in 1766 from the Old Hall in the Cowgate (where they were suffering from the insufficiency of the roof) to the Royal Infirmary, in which they were accommodated for fifteen years, until the Hall in George Street was built, and ready for their reception.

*Printed Catalogue of Drummond Books.*

A printed Catalogue of the Drummond books was presented along with them, and a copy of this Catalogue, still extant, has appended to it the legal documents of conveyance and acceptance, signed in due form. This Catalogue contains a list of 1250 works in all, many of which are no longer in the Library, having in all probability been exchanged, together with other duplicates and non-medical books, in order to enable the College to enlarge its medical collection. Like so many of the books themselves, this copy of the Catalogue had at one period gone astray, and was not recovered till 1820, as appears from an inscription on the title-page, in the handwriting of the late Dr Duncan, Senior, containing an anathema upon any one who should thereafter take it away. On further inquiry, it was found that the College was indebted for its restoration to Mr David Laing, Librarian to the Society of Writers to the Signet, who, on returning it to the Library stated, that he purchased it at a sale of books in Edinburgh; and seeing, from the official documents appended to it in writing, that it had belonged to the Royal College of Physicians, he presented it through the late Dr Wylie, at that time Librarian. Dr Poole has since written on the blank leaves some interesting entries, chiefly taken from the Minutes, calculated to throw light on the fate of this Drummond Collection. It cannot but be deemed a cause of regret that the conditions of the Bequest have been so completely lost sight of, and the Library Committee would gladly have done what was possible towards complying with their spirit, on the occasion of the removal to the Hall in Queen Street in 1846; but, from the great dispersion of the Collection, and the difficulty in replacing the books long since disposed of, which appear from the printed Catalogue to have been partly theological, it was found impossible.

In 1756 a considerable addition to the Library was obtained from Messrs Hamilton and Balfour, booksellers,

*Catalogue of the Drummond Collection lost and recovered.*

*Conditions of Drummond Bequest lost sight of.*

*Books given for Copyright of Pharmacopœia.*

in return for the copyright of the Pharmacopœia published in that year, and for duplicates and other books considered to be unfit for a Medical Library.

*Presentation by Sir Alexander Gibson.*

In 1761 the College was presented with the library of a former Fellow, Dr Edward Wright of Kersie, by Sir Alexander Gibson of Clifton Hall, to whom it had fallen by inheritance. About the same time Dr James Mackenzie, another Fellow, bequeathed to the College seventy-nine quarto volumes, being the Transactions of the Academy of Sciences of Paris from 1666 to 1755.

*Proposal from University for a union with Library declined.*

In 1763 a proposal from the Principal of the University for the union of the Library with the Library of the University, on conditions represented as favourable to the Fellows, came before the College; but after some deliberation, a Report against the proposal was finally adopted. Another proposal to the same effect was made soon after by Dr Robert Whytt, then Professor of the Institutes of Medicine, and a Fellow of the College; but neither was this entertained. In the same year the insurance of the Library is mentioned for the first time, to the amount of £600.

*Books lodged in Infirmary.*

*Donation by Earl of Bute.*

In 1766, owing to the defective condition of the roof of the Old Hall, accommodation, as already noticed, was obtained for the books in the Royal Infirmary. Among the donors to the Library at this period is found John, Earl of Bute, who presented the twenty-six magnificent folios of Sir John Hill's Vegetable System.

*First Catalogue printed in 1767.*

In 1767 the first Catalogue of the Library was printed. This Catalogue, which shows that the Library must have been a large and valuable collection for the period, contains a list of 2346 works. It was printed in 12mo; but there is no notice in the Minutes of the College as to the person by whom it was compiled. Singularly enough, no copy of this interesting little volume had been preserved in the Library, and it was entirely unknown to the Library Committee of 1849, when engaged in preparing the Preface to the Catalogue issued in that year. The College is indebted for the copy now in the Library, probably the only one in existence, to William Brown, Esq., F.R.C.S.E., who, finding it bound up in a volume of pamphlets in his library, lately presented it to the College.

In 1781 the Library was removed from the Infirmary to the New Hall in George Street. In the same year Sir John Pringle presented to the College ten volumes of MS. Annotations, on condition that they were never to be lent out, and never to be published; conditions which have been faithfully adhered to. *Removal to George Street.*

In 1791 the Library Committee were empowered to expend £100 in the purchase of books at the sale of Dr Cullen's library. The new shelving of the Library being by this time completed, a Press Catalogue was prepared, and from it a printed Alphabetical Catalogue was formed, and brought out in 1793. This Catalogue was completed under the care of Dr Thomas Spens, at that time Librarian. In the same year, on the proposal of Dr Duncan, then Professor of the Institutes of Medicine, it was resolved to allow the Professors of the University the privilege of borrowing books from the Library, on condition that the Fellows of the College should enjoy a similar privilege in regard to that of the University. The Senatus Academicus agreed to a trial of this arrangement for one year, but it does not appear to have remained in operation longer. *Purchases at sale of Dr Cullen's Books.*

In 1800 a law was made that all books borrowed should be called in once a year.

In 1801, on the occasion of the retirement of Dr James Home from the office of Librarian, the first notice *Library Committee first appointed.*

appears of the useful practice of appointing a Special Committee to take the Library off the hands of the retiring Librarian, and hand it over to his successor.

In 1821 an Appendix to the Catalogue was printed, containing the additions made to the Library from 1793 to that time.

*Assistant Librarian first appointed.*

In 1823 the appointment of an Assistant Librarian, with a salary, was first resolved on, and Mr John Small was appointed to the office. Up to this time, and indeed throughout the whole history of the Library, much difficulty seems to have been experienced in preventing the books from being taken away in an irregular manner, and in getting the whole of the borrowed books returned.

*Access to University Library refused to Fellows.*

In 1826 the subject of access for the Fellows to the University Library was again agitated, and a Committee was appointed for the furtherance of this object. This Committee continued in existence for nearly four years, and successively memorialised the Patrons of the University, and the Royal Commission on the Scottish Universities, but finally met with a refusal from both.

*Catalogue Raisonnée abandoned.*

In 1826 Dr William Moncrieff was requested to undertake a Catalogue raisonnée of the Library, and in the following year thanks were voted to him for the progress he had made in it. Several years later, after Dr Moncrieff's death, a Committee was formed to prosecute the same object, while Dr William Thomson was Librarian; but after some progress had been made it was relinquished, chiefly because the state of the College funds would not permit of its being printed.

*Dr Andrew Duncan's Bequest.*

In 1828, by the Bequest of Dr Andrew Duncan, Senior, the College came into possession of a large collection of manuscript Notes and Lectures, being the Lectures of the Founders of the Edinburgh School of Medicine, and his own Practical Observations used as

## Historical Sketch.

notes for his Clinical Lectures. The whole collection includes about 180 volumes. A portion of the Practical Observations, however, seems to have been presented by Dr Duncan during his lifetime.

In 1830, on a Report of the Council as to the low state of the funds applicable to the purchase of books, it was resolved that each Fellow should contribute two guineas annually for this purpose. This resolution, however, was suspended almost as soon as passed, and appears in no instance to have been enforced. *(Extraordinary Contribution for Library imposed.)*

In 1831 Dr Walter Adam presented to the Library the twelve folio volumes of Montfauçon's Antiquité Expliquée.

In 1833 Dr Spens presented four Engraved Prints of Medical Practitioners, with a view to make a commencement of a collection of such Prints. The collection is now rapidly increasing, and a list of these Engravings is appended to the Library Catalogue. *(Collection of Prints of Medical Practitioners commenced.)*

In 1835 the Librarian was authorized to have an Appendix to the Library Catalogue printed, but the resolution was not at that time carried into effect.

In 1836 the College, by the Bequest of Dr William Moncrieff, acquired his medical books, consisting of two hundred and twenty-five volumes, of which twenty-one were notes of lectures, etc., in manuscript. *(Dr William Moncrieff's Bequest.)*

In 1844 the Library Committee was empowered, under certain conditions, to make temporary regulations in regard to the Library, owing to the inconvenience arising from the necessity of making a formal application to the College on every new emergency, however trivial.

In 1845 the Library was increased by two considerable donations of books; one by Dr James Home, just before his death, the other by the family of Dr John Abercrombie, after his death. The former consisted of two hundred and forty volumes, including manuscript *(Donations by Dr James Home, and the Family of Dr John Abercrombie.)*

lectures by St Clair, Alston, Cullen, Rutherford, Black, Francis Home, and Gregory. The latter donation comprised about eighty volumes.

*Removal to Queen Street.*

In 1846 the Library, which during the previous three years had been placed in the temporary apartments of the College at 119 George Street, was removed to the New Hall in Queen Street. In the same year, on the occasion of the opening of the New Hall, an important donation to the Library falls to be noticed, consisting of a number of scarce and curious old Medical Books presented by Dr Beilby, who was at that time President.

*Donation by Dr Beilby.*

Immediately upon being settled in the New Hall, the Library Committee took measures for preparing for the press a new Alphabetical Catalogue, and the work was entered upon by the late Mr Small. From the progress made, it was hoped that the printing might have been commenced in the summer of 1847. But unforeseen obstacles were interposed in consequence of the illness and death of Mr Small, and the subsequent illness of the Librarian, who was for a considerable time rendered incapable of superintending the work. In these circumstances the task was taken up by certain members of the Library Committee, who in the end of the year went through the labour of comparing the MS. Catalogue left by Mr Small, with the books themselves, and by great exertions brought the work to a successful termination in 1849.

*New Catalogue commenced.*

*New Catalogue published in 1849.*

Since 1849 the Library has increased very rapidly. By the additional funds placed at its disposal, the Committee have made many valuable additions, particularly in 1852, when they purchased a large portion of the Library of the late Dr John Thomson, Professor of General Pathology in the University of Edinburgh.

*Rapid increase of Library.*

Among the benefactors to the Library, between the

years 1849 and 1854, were Drs Begbie, Bennett, Brown, Jackson, Seller, Robertson, and Simpson.

In 1854 an Appendix to the Catalogue of 1849 was printed, incorporating these additions to the Library.

In 1860, agreeably to an arrangement contemplated by the late Dr John Thomson, there were presented to the College, by Dr Allen Thomson and Dr Craigie, twenty-two volumes of manuscript writings by Dr Cullen; one complete manuscript copy of his Lectures; several editions of his First Lines, especially that by Dr Peter Reid; a German translation of the First Lines, and some smaller articles by the same physician.  *Dr Cullen's MSS. presented.*

All the donations now mentioned, with many others, as well as numerous purchases, have added greatly to the extent of the Library. In the year 1849, when the third edition of the Catalogue was printed, the number of volumes contained in the Library was estimated at about 9000. At present it is calculated that there are in the Library 24,130 volumes.

In order to indicate the progress of the Library, the following statement of the annual additions made to it during the last twelve years is presented:—  *Progress of Library.*

```
1870 ...... 422 volumes were added
1871 ...... 301        ,,         ,,
1872 ...... 314        ,,         ,,
1873 ...... 350        ,,         ,,
1874 ...... 377        ,,         ,,
1875 ...... 397        ,,         ,,
1876 ...... 450        ,,         ,,
1877 ...... 389        ,,         ,,
1878 ...... 432        ,,         ,,
1879 ...... 440        ,,         ,,
1880 ...... 539        ,,         ,,
1881 ...... 612        ,,         ,,

Total ...... 5023 volumes.
```

In 1861 the previous edition of the Catalogue having been all but exhausted, the preparation of a new one was undertaken by Mr John Small, the Assistant Librarian, and by his able management, under the supervision of Dr David Craigie, the President, was completed in about two years. The complete Catalogue was published in a handsome volume in January 1863, and on the 5th May 1863, the sum of £105 was voted to Mr Small for his labours. Since that time two Supplements have been published.

The formation of the Museum of Materia Medica may be dated from the 4th August 1835, when a Committee appointed to consider the sale or improvement of the College Hall in George Street reported—"That it had occurred to the Committee that it might be desirable to commence a Museum of Materia Medica, for the reception of which the Hall, or other part of the building, might gradually, as required, be fitted up." A Committee was appointed to take all measures which should appear to them to be proper for commencing such a Museum.

The Committee accordingly invited the Fellows and others to contribute Donations to the Museum, and entered into a correspondence with Lord Glenelg the Colonial Secretary, and the heads of the Army and Navy Medical Boards, for the purpose of procuring, through their influence, objects of interest for the Museum.

In the meantime Donations began to be received, and the late Dr Davidson had the honour of being the first Contributor, presenting the first three specimens on the 3d November 1835. Dr Christison's Donations were the most numerous and valuable, numbering twenty-nine by April 1837.

The first Honorary Curator, Dr James Stark, appointed in 1839, entered vigorously on the discharge

## Historical Sketch.

of his duties; and it was chiefly through his exertions that the following Donations were obtained:—

In 1839 Dr Christison put the duplicates he might receive for his own collection at the disposal of the College, and became a contributor to the Museum of valuable specimens not otherwise attainable. Mr Duncan (of Duncan and Flockhart), Mr J. F. Macfarlane, and others, also made numerous donations. The Messrs Lawson and Son, on a list being furnished to them of such articles as they could easily procure, kindly presented the collection of cereals and others now in the Museum; and the Botanical Society of Edinburgh, on being furnished with a list of the medicinal plants of Great Britain, generously presented select specimens of the whole, amounting to 338 species, to the Museum of the College. Through the kindness of Professor Graham, and Mr Macnab, the College also obtained from the Royal Botanical Gardens specimens of such medicinal plants as flowered or bore fruit there, and from this source several interesting specimens were procured, and have been preserved both in the green and in the dried states.

To forward the formation of the Museum, Dr James Wood gave a donation of £10, 10s., and the College, from its entertainment fund, gave £25, to be expended in purchase of articles of the Materia Medica. These sums were spent in adding to the Museum 301 specimens, which were placed there on or before the 9th November 1841.

Very few additions were made to the Museum from the above date till 1847, when the College, having heard that Dr Theodore Martius of Erlangen, the brother of the celebrated Brazilian traveller, wished to dispose of his splendid and very complete collection of Materia Medica, resolved to purchase it. After considerable correspondence, it was announced to the College at its meeting on the 3d August 1847, that Dr Martius' collection had been secured for the College for the sum of £250. Through the influence of Sir William Gibson-Craig, then M.P. for Edinburgh and one of the Lords of the Treasury, the whole collection was not only passed free of duty, but was allowed to be forwarded to the College Hall before being opened.

No time was lost in getting suitable cases and show-tables fitted up for the exhibition of this collection, and on the 1st of May 1848 the Martius' Collection was arranged and ready for inspection.

| | |
|---|---:|
| The Animal Preparations in this collection amount to | 160 |
| Vegetable do., . . . . . | 1395 |
| Mineral do., . . . . | 309 |
| TOTAL, | 1864 |

During the years 1848, 1849, and 1850, the Museum received a valuable addition in the form of a complete series of Cinchona and allied Barks, presented by John Elliot Howard, Esq. of Tottenham. This series embraced specimens of all the Barks met with in British commerce, and also a series of the Lichens growing on the Barks.

*Present state of Museum.*

On a rough calculation, the preparations in the Museum may be arranged as follows:—

| | |
|---|---:|
| Animal Preparations, . | 166 |
| Vegetable do., | 2163 |
| Mineral do., | 380 |
| TOTAL, | 2709 |

*Proposed Gift of Collection of Materia Medica to Museum of Science and Art.*

When the Museum of Science and Art was established by Government, some idea existed of presenting this Collection to it. This, however, was set at rest by a

Report from a Committee on increased Library Accommodation, which was drawn up by a Committee, of which Dr Christison was chairman, and unanimously adopted by the College on 18th November 1862. The following Excerpt relates to the Museum:—

"It was next suggested, that time might be given for beginning the extension of the Hall, by converting the present Museum room into a Library room, which would provide for the increase of books for a period of ten years at least. For this purpose it would be necessary to part with the Museum of Materia Medica; and it was further suggested that the Museum might be presented to the Museum of Science and Art, or the University, where it would be more accessible, and more widely visited than in Physicians' Hall. The Committee resolved, however, almost unanimously, to recommend the College, if possible, not to part with the Museum. The Museum and Cases, together with the special embellishment of the apartment cost the College about £750. The Collection is a unique one in this country, being an almost complete Collection of the 'Medicamina Simplicia' of the Materia Medica, as it stood at the time of its purchase from Dr Martius of Erlangen; and as the specimens are choice and in excellent order, the Collection will always be an object of interest on this historical ground, even although the College should never add to it. The Committee, indeed, are assured that it is a subject of interest to strangers, and that its existence in the College is well known to the cultivators of Materia Medica. They do not think that the College would willingly part with a Collection which cost them so much, and which brings the College some credit. The Committee have come to the resolution to recommend the retention of the Museum, all the more willingly, because they see a plan for leaving it untouched, for obtaining increased Library Accommodation, and for extending the Hall without delay, by a single scheme which will not unduly encroach on the College Funds."

*Report of Committee as to Museum.*

It has been thought advisable to conclude this short sketch of the History of the College, by a brief summary of some of the more interesting or more important Minutes of the College.

*First Meetings, 7th, 8th, and 9th December 1681.*

The first two Meetings of the College (*7th and 8th December* 1681) were occupied with the election of Office Bearers. Immediately thereafter they proceeded (*9th December* 1681), under the powers vested in them by the Charter, "to enact Laws for its due government and welfare." It is exceedingly interesting to find, that, in addition to fixing the number necessary to constitute a quorum, the two Laws then enacted have continued in force to the present time. The one provides that every new Law shall be considered at two separate Meetings of the College before being enacted, and that every proposal to abrogate a Law shall be considered at three several Meetings before a decision is come to; the other, that every proposal before being laid before the College, "shall be represented to the President and Council, who shall take it into consideration, and report the same at the next Meeting of the College, with the sense of the Council thereupon."

*Bye Laws.*

*Period of election of Office Bearers.*

*4th and 18th January* 1682.—Nearly as early in the history of the College, the day for the election of the Office Bearers, and the periods at which the Quarterly Meetings were to be held, were fixed, and these, too, have continued unaltered to the present time.

*Fines.*

*10th February* 1682.—At these Meetings, fines of "*seri*" (coming one quarter after the hour of meeting) and "*absentes,*" are first mentioned, although, as the time for collecting them only is fixed, it seems probable that they had been inflicted previously.

*Promissory Engagements.*

*21st March* 1682.—The draught of the promissory engagement, to be signed by Fellows on taking their seats, was agreed to.

*Resolutions.*

*3d November* 1684.—A Committee was appointed "to

## Historical Sketch.

revise all former Acts, and to order the booking of such of them as they shall think fit in the Great Register."

*6th January* 1685.—The Committee appointed to revise the Laws reported. They first proposed a regulation for the minimum course of study for the Licence; next for the trial of Apothecaries, suggesting that none should be permitted to officiate as Apothecaries until they had been examined "upon their skill in the Simples, in the Latin tongue, reading of receipts, and what else shall be found needful." Rules for Examination of Licentiates and Apothecaries.

From *22d November* 1684 to *21st March* 1693, a blank occurs in the Minutes; and during that period, and for some time thereafter, the College would appear to have been chiefly occupied with the discussions between it and the Chirurgeon Apothecaries, and the legal proceedings consequent upon them. Blank in Minutes from 22d December 1684 to 21st March 1693.

*9th November* 1693.—The Fees to be paid by Fellows and Licentiates were fixed. Fees.

It would appear that a custom had prevailed of the whole College electing the President. It was, however, proposed and discussed at two Meetings, and passed into an Act (*14th November* 1695), that the seven Councillors chosen by the College should elect one of their number to be President, and this notwithstanding any custom to the contrary; and this Law, which indeed seems to have been compulsory by the Charter, continued in force until the first Bye-Laws under the new Charter of 1860, were passed. Election of President.

*26th August,* 1701.—The Fees of admission of Fellows and Licentiates were again altered. Fees.

*12th January* 1704.—A Committee was named to revise the Laws.

*6th May* 1707.—An Act was passed to render more effectual the separation between the Physician and Surgeon. It was ordained that this Act should be signed by all the Fellows. This would appear to have been done; and, subsequently, each Fellow at his entrance would seem to have signed it up to 1756, when the practice was discontinued, but without any notice of its discontinuance in the Minutes. Act for separation between Physician and Surgeon.

For some time subsequently to this, various Acts were passed regulating the "dues of Entrants and Licentiates," but nothing of particular interest occurs until—

*No Fellow to keep a Shop.*

6*th November* 1750.—When an Act was unanimously passed, prohibiting the admission of any one as a Fellow of the College who was a Member of the Corporation of Surgeons or Apothecaries, or who kept a shop for the dispensing of Medicine, and declaring that any one doing so after his admission "shall, *ipso facto*, forfeit all privileges which he did, or might, enjoy as a Fellow of the College, and his name shall be expunged out of the Roll of Fellows."

11*th April* 1754.—A farther Act to prevent the same person from conjoining the professions of Medicine and Pharmacy was read a third time, and passed unanimously.

*Candidates for Fellowship to be Licentiates for one year.*

1*st November* 1763.—An Act was read a third time, and passed, "that in all time coming every Doctor of Medicine should remain a Licentiate one whole year before becoming a Fellow; that no Member of the Corporation of Surgeons should be admitted a Fellow or Licentiate, and that any Licentiate or Fellow becoming a Member of the said Corporation should forfeit his Licence or Fellowship."

*No Fellow to keep an Apothecary's shop.*

1*st May* 1764.—On the Report of a Committee, the College confirmed its former Act (11*th April* 1754) in regard to Fellows keeping Apothecaries' shops, and extended it to all residing in Great Britain and Ireland, declaring that any Fellow of the College practising Pharmacy within the three kingdoms, should, *ipso facto*, forfeit his right of Fellowship, and his name should be struck off from the Roll of Fellows.

*No Fellow to practise Surgery or Midwifery.*

17*th May* 1765.—An Act was passed declaring that for the future no person should be admitted to be one of the Fellows, "whose common business it is either to practise Surgery in general, or Midwifery, Lithotomy, Inoculation, or any other branch of it in particular; and further, that if any Member of the College shall, after his being received a Fellow, practise any of these lower acts in the manner above-mentioned, and shall thereof be lawfully convicted, he shall be degraded from the honour conferred upon him when he was admitted a Fellow, and his name shall be struck out of the Roll."

*7th February* 1769.—After full consideration by a Committee, and repeated discussion in the College, an Act was passed providing that no Fellow or Licentiate of the College should exercise the business or profession of Midwifery, Lithotomy, or any of the other manual operations of Surgery; and providing, that if lawfully convicted, he should be fined 40 pounds Scots for the first offence, and for the second, if convicted, he should forfeit his right of Fellowship, if a Fellow of the College, or his right of Licence, if a Licentiate, and all right and title whatever to practise physic within the city of Edinburgh and Liberties thereof.

*7th November* 1769.—The Act of *7th February* was rescinded.

*5th May* 1770.—A motion to rescind the Act *17th May* 1765, was rejected.

*5th February* 1771.—An Act was passed for henceforth balloting for Candidates for the Fellowship.

*6th August* 1772.—The Act of *17th May* 1765, was amended on the Report of a Committee to whom it had been remitted for consideration.

*4th August* 1772.—The Act prohibiting Fellows from practising Surgery or Midwifery was renewed, and it was ordained that all Fellows doing so, and against whom it should be fully proved, should forfeit their Fellowship, and their name should be struck out of the Roll.

*3d November* 1773.—The number of Honorary Fellows was restricted to ten.

*24th February* 1774.—Professors of Universities having by the Charter a right to be admitted Honorary Fellows, it was resolved that in any lists of Fellows thereafter published, such Honorary Fellows, *ex officio*, "shall be distinguished by some proper mark from those admitted by the voluntary act of the College"

*4th November* 1783.—The form of petition for Non-Resident Fellows was altered.

*Graduates of Foreign Universities.*

*8th June* 1784.—An Act was passed permitting the Graduates of Foreign Universities to be admitted Fellows without examination, on a motion to that effect being proposed at one Quarterly Meeting, and duly determined by ballot at the next.

*Repeal of Act against Fellows practising Midwifery.*

*6th May* 1788.—The College repealed the Resolution of *4th August* 1772, "in so far as it prohibits the Fellows of the College from the practice of Midwifery."

Hitherto the Laws and Regulations of the College are to be gathered only from the Minute-Books. It is apparent, however, that a growing desire began to be felt that these Laws should be digested into one body or code, and printed. In this matter the College appears to have acted with becoming caution and consideration, for on the

*Abstract of Laws to be prepared.*

*2d November* 1784, a Committee was appointed for the purpose of preparing an Abstract of the Laws enacted from *7th December* 1681 to *3d August* 1784. This Committee reported on the *2d May* 1786, when the matter was re-committed to be further considered and completed.

*1st August and 7th November* 1786.—From statements made at these Meetings, it would appear that the Committee was not yet prepared finally to report.

*6th February* 1787.—The Report of the Committee was laid on the table, ordered to be printed, and circulated among the Fellows.

*1st May* 1787.—A motion approving of the Report was read a first and a second time.

*First Edition of Laws.*

*6th November* 1787.—Some delay was now interposed, until the question of the repeal of the Law preventing Fellows from practising Midwifery was settled. This Law having been repealed on the *5th August* 1788, the College, at the first Quarterly Meeting thereafter (*4th November* 1788), unanimously approved of the Laws as proposed, "sanctioned and established the same, and resolved that the Laws should be printed as amended." Thus the first Code of Laws was arranged and printed in the year 1789. Copies of this little volume are still extant.

Soon after changes were introduced, and, on the 2d *February* 1790, it was enacted—

*First,* That when two or more Licentiates were elected Fellows at the same Meeting, they should be marked on the Roll according to the date of their admission ; and if they were of the same date as Licentiates, they should be enrolled according to the date of their Diplomas ; and if their Diplomas were of the same date, they should be enrolled according to their age. *(Order of Seniority.)*

*Second.*—That any Law of the College might be suspended for a limited time, provided said suspension was agreed to by two-thirds of the Fellows present, and that due intimation of the proposal was made in the Billets by which the Fellows were summoned. *(Suspension of a Law.)*

*3d August* 1790.—To secure the strict enforcement of the payment of fines, it was ordered that absentees at the last Meeting should be called on to pay their fines immediately after the roll-call, and Fellows who were late, to pay the fines as they came in. *(Payment of Fines.)*

*6th August* 1793.—The Entrance-Fee of Resident Fellows was fixed at £100 *net*. *(Entrance Fee.)*

*2d February* 1796.—A proposal was made to repeal the Act dated 11*th April* 1754, in so far that every Fellow or Licentiate of the College might have it in his power to supply his own patients with medicines, or the patients of those with whom he might be conjoined in practice. This motion was read a second time 3*d May* 1796, and a third time 2*d August* 1796, when the discussion was adjourned, to be resumed 1*st November* 1796, and again adjourned. *(Discussions in regard to Fellows supplying Medicine.)*

The proceedings connected with this gave rise to a most painful personal dissension between some of the most eminent Fellows, the discussions on which appear to have occupied much of the Minutes at that time. All these Minutes were, however, erased by an order of the College, dated 4*th May* 1830. Enough, however, is still to be found in the volumes printed on the subject, Dr James Gregory's Censorial Letter ;

Dr Andrew Duncan's Opinion on a Charge against Dr James Gregory, 4to, Ed. 1808; Dr Andrew Duncan's Letter to Dr Gregory, 8vo Ed. 1811; Narrative of the Conduct of Dr James Gregory, published by authority of the Royal College of Physicians, 4to, Edin. 1809.

On the *4th August* 1795, another attempt to enforce the rigid collection of the fines was made, and the reason of this became apparent on *2d May* 1797, when the contributions and fines not being sufficient to defray the expenses of the entertainments, the College resolved that in future £5 be paid by each Fellow towards them.

*7th February* 1804.—A Committee was appointed to revise the Laws with a view to a new edition being issued. This Committee reported progress *1st May* 1804, and laid a copy of their Report before the College *7th August* 1804.

The Report was considered in *November*, and again in *February*, when, in consequence of much difference of opinion, it was (*5th February* 1805) re-committed. The amended Report having been brought up (*7th May* 1805), the first reading engaged the attention of the College at no fewer than four Meetings. The Laws, however, were finally read a third time and adopted (*2d September* 1805), not however, without a protest.

*5th November* 1805.—It having been stated that the copy of the promissory engagement signed by each Fellow on taking his seat was irretrievably lost, the Clerk was directed to prepare a new one.

*4th February* 1806.—The new edition of the Laws in print was laid on the table. A new promissory engagment was produced and signed by those present.

*6th May* 1823.—The Council of the College was appointed a Committee for the purpose of revising the Laws of the College, with a view to the printing of a new edition.

*6th May* 1823.—The Act of 1754, as far as it regarded the practice of Surgery, was totally repealed, and that part of it relating to the practice of Pharmacy altered as follows:—" If any Fellow or Licentiate of the College shall, by himself, co-partner, or servants, keep a public Apothecary's, Druggist's, or Chemist's shop, he shall, *ipso facto*, forfeit all the rights and privileges which he does, or may, enjoy as a Fellow or Licentiate of the said College, and his name shall be expunged from the List."

*3d August* 1824.—The Committee appointed, *6th May* 1823, laid on the table proof copies of the Revised Laws; these were considered at no fewer than eleven Meetings of the College, but were never finally adopted.

*5th August* 1828.—The President having reported that the edition of the Laws, 1805, was exhausted, it was agreed that the Laws which had been in proof for four years should be again revised, for which purpose a Committee was appointed.

*4th November* 1828.—The Report of the Committee on the Laws was given in; it was ordered to be printed and circulated among the Fellows.

*4th August* 1829—The Laws and Regulations of the College as amended were finally adopted.

*1st February* 1831.—It was agreed that any Fellow leaving the room during a meeting of the College should be fined.

*3d May* 1831.—A motion was carried, regulating the Fees for the Licence and Fellowship.

*7th August* 1832.—It was resolved that the ballot for the admission of Ordinary Resident Fellows might take place at the Quarterly Meeting following the presentation of their petition, in the same way as in the case of Non-Resident Fellows.

*5th November* 1833.—A Motion for the infliction of Fines upon the Members of the Council of the College for non-attendance was agreed to.

*1st August* 1837.—A Letter was read from a Fellow of the College, proposing that for the future Candidates for the Licence and Fellowship should not be required to possess Medical Degrees, but that provision should be otherwise made for ascertaining their Qualifications. This subject occupied much of the time of the College, and gave rise to much discussion at many subsequent Meetings. At the succeeding Meeting

*7th November* 1837, A Committtee was appointed to consider and report upon it

*Legal Opinion*

*7th February* 1838.—The Report of this Committee was given in, along with the Opinion of Mr John Hope, Dean of the Faculty of Advocates, and Mr James Ivory, Advocate, on certain Queries submitted to them regarding it. The remit to the Committee was continued, that they might report farther on the matter.

*Fees not returned where a Fellow elected died before taking his seat.*

*19th May* 1838.—In consequence of the death of a gentleman who had been balloted for, and admitted a Fellow of the College, but who died before taking his seat, a question arose as to whether his fees of admission should be returned to his heirs. The College resolved that money so paid was the property of the College, and could not be alienated unless in the manner prescribed by law for the alienation of other property.

*18th December* 1838.—The Report of the Committee on the admission of Fellows was again considered, and the final decision on it postponed.

*20th February* 1839.—The Report of a Committee on the admission of Fellows was again considered. Two motions were made:—1st, Motion to approve of the Report. 2d, Motion to disapprove. The vote being taken, the second Motion was carried by the casting vote of the President.

*Draught of New Charter.*

*21st March* 1843.—The draught of a proposed new Charter for the College was read and approved of. Owing to the prospect continually held out of some measure of Medical Reform being adopted by the Legislature, by which the Charters of all existing bodies would be altered, no farther steps were taken to procure this new Charter for the College.

*Trustees.*

*1st August* 1843.—Resolved that all property belonging to the College should be invested in Trustees to be chosen by the Council, with the approval of the College. The Trustees to be five in number, of whom the Treasurer should be one *ex officio.*

*7th November* 1843.—Certain regulations for the examination of Foreign Graduates, which had been several times under the consideration of the College, were read a third time, and passed.  *Foreign Graduates.*

*4th November* 1846.—A motion that an official costume should be worn by the Fellows, was read a second time, and negatived.

*4th May* 1847.—Resolved that as full a notice as possible of the business to be transacted at the Meetings of the College be given in the Billets by which the Meeting was summoned.

*4th May* 1847.—Report of Committee on the examination of Fellows proposing to deliver Lectures on the subjects required by Examining Medical Boards, laid on the table.  *Certificate required of Fellows proposing to Lecture.*

*2d November* 1847.—Regulations in regard to the examination of Fellows proposing to Lecture finally adopted, after being discussed at Meetings held *11th* and *14th May*, and *3d August*, 1847.

*1st August* 1848.—Resolved that the book containing the record of examination of Foreign Graduates should not henceforth be laid on the table, but only a copy of the entry regarding the examination of successful Candidates.

*5th November* 1850.—Moved that a Committee be appointed to revise the Laws, and to report to the Council such suggestions for their improvement as might appear to them desirable; and that the Council, after full consideration of these suggestions, should report them to the College, with their opinion thereon.  *Revision of Laws.*

*5th August* 1851.—The new Laws, as considered by the Council, were laid on the table, and the following motion was unanimously adopted—" That, as it is extremely desirable that no Law should be adopted until it has received the fullest possible consideration, the College do now resolve that all proposed amendments on the Laws be given in to the Secretary, in writing, within ten days, and be thereafter considered by the Council and Law Committee conjointly, who shall Report them, with their opinion thereon, at next Meeting of the College."  *Revision of new Laws.*

It was farther resolved, That the amendments to be proposed, with the Opinion of the Council and Committee thereon, should be printed, and circulated among the Fellows previous to the Meeting at which they are to be discussed.

*4th May* 1852.—The new Laws were considered for the third time, and agreed to.

*2d November* 1852.—Standing Order regulating the manner in which Fellows were to take their seats, unanimously adopted.

*2d August* 1853.—The College agreed to petition Parliament on behalf of the Assistant Surgeons of the Royal Navy.

Dr George Paterson presented to the College a Digested Index of its Proceedings for the first fifty years of its existence, for which he received the "warm thanks" of the College.

*1st November* 1855.—Mr Craig, Surgeon, Ratho, presented to the College the cane which had belonged to, and had been used by, the late Dr Cullen.

*9th May* 1854.—A Committee appointed for the purpose, presented a Report on the Bill for the Registration of Births, Deaths, and Marriages. The College adopted the Report, and petitioned in favour of the Bill.

*7th August* 1855.—A Committee reported on the expediency of having a Meteorological Society established in Scotland.

*5th August* 1856.—A Committee reported in favour of the College offering a Prize for competition. Motion to that effect read a first time.

*14th November* 1856.—The College resolved that at the Election Meeting Fellows should vote by signed lists instead of *viva voce*, as heretofore.

*3d February* 1857.—Resolutions in regard to the position of the Army Medical Service agreed to, and ordered to be transmitted to the Secretary at War.

*3d February* 1857.—The College agreed to a motion offering a Prize of Twenty-Five Guineas for an Essay.

*21st July* 1857.—The College considered the Lunacy

(Scotland) Bill then before Parliament, and adopted certain resolutions regarding it,—in particular the College agreed to suggest and recommend the "Emergency Clause," which has since become Law.

*3d November* 1857.—Power was granted to the Council to withhold inspection of the Minutes of the Council as to any particular piece of business still in dependence. Minutes of Council to be private in certain circumstances.

*2d February* 1858.—The College agreed to have the State of the Accounts and Funds of the College printed and circulated annually.

*9th April* 1858.—The College memorialized the Board of Trade to grant some pecuniary aid to the Meteorological Society of Scotland. Meteorological Society.

*20th July* 1858.—The College agreed to entertain the Members of the British Medical Association, then about to visit Edinburgh. Entertainment to British Association.

*21st September* 1858.—The College resolved to publish annually a complete list of the Fellows. List of Fellows to be annually published.

*21st December* 1858.—The College resolved to apply for a new Charter.

*1st February* 1859.—The Trustees submitted to the College the Opinion of Mr Maitland, Advocate (afterwards Lord Barcaple), as to the nature of the Investments which they were warranted in availing themselves of for placing the funds of the College. Legal Opinion to College Investments.

*8th February* 1859.—The College resolved that the funds be withdrawn from investments in companies where a liability might exist for sums beyond those invested.

A Committee was appointed to consider the best means of accommodating the rapidly increasing Library.

The College altered the Laws relating to the election of the Council, and decided that the voting papers should not be signed.

An application from certain Non-Resident Fellows was read, desiring to be admitted to participate in the government of the College.

*18th February* 1859.—The College agreed to a Memorial to the Chancellor of the Exchequer, praying for relief from the Stamp Duties on the Licence of the College. It was resolved to join with the London and Dublin Colleges of Physicians in sending a deputation to London on the subject.

*1st March* 1859.—The draft of the new Charter, with the Opinion of Mr Roundell Palmer (afterwards Lord Chancellor Selborne), was farther considered, and ultimately agreed to.

*8th March* 1859.—The College, on a Report by the Council, resolved to petition in favour of the "Sale of Poisons Bill;" it also resolved not to interfere in regard to two Lunacy Bills which appeared to refer to England exclusively.

*29th March* 1859.—The President refused to allow the business of an Extraordinary Meeting, called by requisition, to proceed, because the requisitionists had failed to submit their proposed Motion to the Council previously, as required by the Laws of the College.

*5th April* 1859.—The College, by a majority of one, resolved to admit to examination as Candidates for its Licence, gentlemen who had no previous Medical Degree or Qualification.

*20th April* 1859.—The Regulations for the examination and admission of Candidates for the Licence were finally agreed to, after having been discussed at many previous Meetings of the College.

*14th June* 1859.—The Council gave in a Report on the Stamp Duties on the Diplomas of Licentiates, which, through the exertions of the President, Dr Alexander Wood, the Lords of Her Majesty's Treasury had agreed to remit.

The College resolved to revise the Laws, and bring them into conformity with the proposed Charter.

*15th June* 1859.—The Council announced that by the exertions of the President, Dr Alexander Wood, the English Poor Law Board had agreed to recognise the Licence of the College as a Medical Qualification.

*Historical Sketch.*

*26th July* 1859.—The College agreed to certain Regulations for giving a Double Qualification along with the Royal College of Surgeons, by a single examination, to be submitted for the approval of the next Meeting of the General Council of Medical Education.

*27th September* 1859.—The College agreed to a Minute recording their sense of the loss the community had sustained by the death of Dr William Pulteney Alison, and resolved to attend his funeral as a Body.

Professor Allen Thomson of Glasgow, with consent of the direct descendants of Dr Cullen who were in this country, presented to the College the manuscripts left by the late Dr Cullen, consisting of about fifteen volumes in folio and twenty in quarto, with about an equal number of loose papers.

*7th February* 1860.—The College resolved to procure for the Hall a marble bust of the late Professor Alison.

It was agreed to send Delegates to a conference with the Colleges of Physicians of London and Dublin, with a view to securing some uniformity in the Charters to be granted to the three Bodies.

*29th March* 1860.—The College agreed to co-operate with the London and Dublin Colleges in having a Bill introduced into Parliament to abolish the 47th clause of the Medical Act, and to leave to Bodies obtaining new Charters the privileges they possessed at the time of passing of the Medical Act.

The College granted the use of the Hall to the Senatus Academicus of the University, for the purpose of entertaining the Chancellor of the Exchequer (The Right Honourable W. E. Gladstone) at dinner, on occasion of his Installation as Rector of the University, but carefully guarded against this being construed into a precedent.

*1st May* 1860.—The College unanimously adopted a Report from a Committee appointed on the 1st February, to consider in what manner the College should mark its sense of the services rendered to it by the President, and agreed to the recommendation of the Committee, that the College should present him with his portrait, painted by an Artist of high eminence, and that, on the condition of adequate eminence, the choice of the Artist should be with Dr Wood himself.'

*1st May* 1860.—The Council, at the request of the University Commissioners, reported on the Ordinances which were proposed in regard to conferring Degrees in Medicine.

*14th May* 1860. — The College resolved to entertain at Dinner Lord Brougham, Chancellor of the University, Drs Watson and Sharpey of London, and Dr Stokes of Dublin, who were to receive the degree of LL.D. from the University.

The College recalled a Licence on account of a false statement of age having been made.

*19th June* 1860.—The College agreed to invite the Officers of the Channel Fleet, lying at St Margaret's Hope, to an entertainment.

*3d August* 1860.—The College resolved to alter the day on which the next Quarterly Meeting of the College should have been held to the day following (first Wednesday in August 1860), inasmuch as the former had been fixed upon by Her Majesty to review the Volunteers.

*6th November* 1860.—The College resolved to reduce the fees payable by Fellows on entrance.

*5th February* 1861.—The College presented the President, Dr Alexander Wood, with his portrait, painted by Sir John Watson Gordon, President of the Royal Academy.

The Council reported in regard to the new Charter, and recommended the College to retain the name of the College of Physicians of Edinburgh, instead of assuming that of the College of Physicians of Scotland, to which it was entitled by the Medical Act. This was agreed to by the College.

*7th May* 1861.—The Council reported a correspondence between the President and the War Office, and also the proceedings at a conference between the President, a Delegate from the Royal College of Surgeons of Edinburgh, and Lord

Herbert, Secretary-at-War, in regard to the recognition of the Double Qualification by the Army Medical Board.

The Council reported a correspondence between the Secretary of the College, and the Poor Law Board of England, in regard to the recognition by the Board of the Double Qualification as equivalent to a Degree in Medicine and a Degree in Surgery. *(Negotiation with Poor Law Board.)*

*5th November* 1861.—The President laid before the College the new Charter, dated 16th August, and sealed 31st October 1861. *(New Charter laid before College.)*

*20th December* 1861.—The College agreed to an Address of Condolence to the Queen on the death of the Prince Consort. *(Address to the Queen on death of Prince Consort.)*

*4th February* 1862.—The Address to the Queen, and Reply, were reported to the College.

*25th June* 1862.—The College voted twenty-five guineas towards the subscription for a National Memorial to the late Prince Consort. *(Vote to Albert Memorial.)*

The petition of a Lady to be allowed to pass the Preliminary Examination with a view to taking the Licence of the College, was, on a division, rejected. *(Lady refused to be admitted to Preliminary Examination.)*

*11th July* 1862.—The College resolved that the Bye-Laws, which had been repeatedly under the consideration of the College, should be the Statutes and Bye-Laws of the College, by which it should be governed and directed,—these Laws were ordered to be printed. *(New Bye-Laws agreed to.)*

*25th October* 1862.—The College agreed to a resolution recommending the Medical Council to adopt the Decimal System of Weights and Measures in the forthcoming British Pharmacopœia. *(Recommend Decimal System of Weights.)*

*4th November* 1862.—The Council reported to the College the neglected state of the Tomb of the late Dr Cullen, in Kirknewton burial-ground, and recommended the College to erect some memorial to his memory. *(Dr Cullen's Tomb.)*

*27th November* 1862.—The College took up the case of a Licentiate accused of advertising in an improper way, and of publishing an indecent quasi-medical book. The Licentiate *(Case of a Licentiate accused of advertising.)*

appeared by his Procurator, who emitted a declaration in presence of a Justice of the Peace, which set forth, *inter alia*, that his name was inserted in the advertisements and on the title page of the publication complained of, without his authority and against his remonstrance. On this the College delayed proceedings.

An Address to the Queen on the Prince of Wales attaining his majority was agreed to, and directed to be forwarded for presentation.

*3d February* 1863.—The College resolved to request Mr Whyte Melville of Mount Melville, to allow the portrait of his grandfather Dr Whytt, to be copied for the College.

*31st March* 1863.—The College agreed to present an Address of Congratulation to the Queen on the marriage of the Prince of Wales, and also one to the Prince of Wales.

*5th May* 1863.—A bust of the late Professor Gregory was presented by Dr Keiller to the College.

The Council reported on the state of the grave of the late Dr Cullen, and the College voted £100 to carry out their recommendations.

*7th July* 1863.—A motion was made to remove the name of a Licentiate from the Roll for having published an indecent quasi-medical work. The College agreed to entertain it.

*4th August* 1863.—The College agreed to approve of changes proposed in the duration of the Session of the University.

The College agreed to entertain at Dinner the President and leading Members of the Social Science Congress, about to be held in Edinburgh.

*12th October* 1863.—The College entertained at Dinner, in their Hall, His Royal Highness Prince Alfred, attended by Major Cowell; Lord Brougham; The Right Honourable Charles Lawson, Lord Provost; The Right Honourable W. E. Gladstone, Chancellor of the Exchequer; The Right Honourable Joseph Napier, M.P.; Sir Christopher Rawlinson; Sir Harry Young, K.C.B.; Sir J. Kay Shuttleworth, Bart.;

## Historical Sketch.

Sir Charles Hastings; Judge Longfield; Sir David Brewster; John Pender, M.P.; Nassau Senior, Esq.; John Thomson Gordon, Esq., Sheriff of the County of Edinburgh; Dr Newbigging, President of the Royal College of Surgeons; Mr William Brougham; M. Garnier Pages; M. Desmaret; M. Henri Martin; M. Herold; Professors Syme, Maclagan, Lyon Playfair, and Archer; Colonel Torrens; the Rev. Dr Bell of Goole; Messrs Whyte Melville, E. Chadwick, Westlake, R. Rawlinson, W. Cookson, Hastings, H. Roberts, A. Kinnear, and Dr Markham.  *Dinner to Social Science Congress.*

Apologies were received from His Grace the Duke of Buccleuch; Earls Russell and Minto; Lord Dunfermline; the Lord Justice-General (M'Neill), the Lord Advocate (Moncreiff), the Lord Justice-Clerk (Inglis); Lords Currichill, Neaves, and Ardmillan; Sir Walter Crofton, Sir John M'Neill, G.C.B., Sir William Gibson-Craig, Bart.; Hon. M. Waldegrave Leslie; Bishop Morell; Captains Speke and Grant; Adam Black, M.P.  *Letters of Apology.*

*3d November* 1863.—The College resolved to obtain portraits of Drs Christison and Seller.  *Portraits of Drs Christison and Seller to be obtained.*

A Licentiate of the College was deprived of his Licence for publishing an indecent quasi-medical work.

*2d February* 1864.—The College agreed to Congratulatory Addresses to the Queen and Prince of Wales on the occasion of the birth of the Prince Royal.  *Congratulation on birth of Prince Royal.*

The College, on the suggestion of the Council, remitted to the Council to procure a portrait of Sir Alexander Morison, the oldest Fellow of the College.  *Portrait of Sir Alexander Morison to be procured.*

The College agreed to a series of resolutions explaining to the Fellows, Members, and Licentiates, their duties under the Vaccination (Scotland) Act.  *Duties under Vaccination Act.*

*19th February* 1865.—The College adopted certain resolutions in regard to the protection of Medical men signing Certificates of Lunacy.

*22d March* 1865.—A Report of a Committee on Improvements on Medical Education was read and discussed.

Purchase of No. 8 Queen Street, the house adjoining the College on the east, by the Trustees for £6000, was announced.

*3d May* 1864.—The Committee formerly appointed, reported the Answers which they recommended the College to send to the Resolutions and Recommendations on General and Professional Education, issued by the General Council of Medical Education and Registration in June 1863.

The College remitted to the Council to consider the present state of the Army Medical Department, and especially the offer made to Civilians to enter for temporary service.

The College approved of a letter dated 26th March 1864, addressed by the President to the Home Secretary, pointing out the prevalence of small-pox in the Western Highlands, and the want of facilities for procuring supplies of vaccine lymph.

*2d August.*—A Committee was appointed to consider the extension of accommodation for the Library.

A scheme for the formation of Scholarships, prepared by a Committee in conjunction with the Council of the College, was approved of, and £25 *per annum* was voted from the College funds to carry it on.

A report of conferences with the College of Surgeons and Glasgow Faculty on the Education Report of the General Medical Council, was approved of.

Sir Alexander Morison made over to the College the lands of Larchgrove, in the County of Edinburgh, the proceeds to be devoted to the salary of a Lecturer on Mental Diseases, Sir Alexander naming Dr William Seller as the first Lecturer.

The College negatived a motion to make the offices of Secretary and Treasurer paid offices; but remitted to the Council to consider the expediency of appointing a Fellow to manage the applications for the Licence of the College, and the conditions on which the office should be established.

*18th November* 1864.—The College agreed to a plan of Library accommodation, by which the Hall was to be extended to double its present size, and surrounded with low book-cases.

## Historical Sketch.

*7th February* 1865.—The College resolved to have a copy executed of a portrait of a former President, Dr John Clark, in the possession of Hugh H. Brown, Esquire of Newhall, whose permission for this had been obtained. *[Portrait of Dr John Clark.]*

The College granted the use of the Hall for an entertainment to be given by the President (Dr Burt) to the Fellows. *[Entertainment by Dr Burt to Fellows.]*

*2d May* 1865.—The College, on the recommendation of the Council made in obedience to a remit from the College (1st November 1864), agreed to appoint a Registrar whose duty should be the management of the applications for the Licence of the College; the Council to elect annually to the office, and to have the power of conjoining it with the office of Secretary, or of separating the two offices at any time, as might seem most expedient. *[Appointment of a Registrar.]*

*7th November* 1865.—The College, on the recommendation of the Council, agreed to adopt a Collegiate costume, and remitted to the Council to determine what the costume should be. *[Adoption of a Collegiate costume.]*

*6th March* 1866.—The College expressed its approval of the action of the Municipal Authorities in inaugurating a comprehensive scheme of Sanitary Reform. *[Approval of Municipal Scheme of Sanitary Reform.]*

*10th April* 1866.—The College approved of the Report of the Council on the Lunacy Acts (Scotland) Bill then before Parliament. *[Lunacy Acts (Scotland) Bill.]*

*21st May* 1866.—The College agreed to petition Parliament to the effect that two Representatives in Parliament at least, be granted to the Scottish Universities. *[Petition in favour of University Representation.]*

*7th May* 1867.—College resolved to petition in favour of the Public Health (Scotland) Bill, which had been introduced into Parliament. *[Petition in favour of Public Health Bill.]*

*4th February* 1868.—The College approved of the Report of the Council, on the recommendations of the General Medical Council, on the subjects of Preliminary Examinations of Medical Students, and on the Report of the Committee on the Visitation of Examinations. *[Preliminary Examination and Visitation of Examinations.]*

A copy of a portrait of Dr Arbuthnot was presented to the College by Dr Seller. *[Portrait of Dr Arbuthnot.]*

*18th February* 1868.—The College voted the sum of £1000 in aid of the fund for the buildings of the New Royal Infirmary.

*5th May* 1868.—The College agreed to present an Address to the Queen with reference to the attempted assassination of the Duke of Edinburgh; also to his Royal Highness, congratulating him on his providential escape.

The College agreed to purchase, for the sum of £100, a bust, by Maccallum, of the deceased Dr John Graham Macdonald Burt, lately President of the College.

The College recommended that the Maternity Hospital should be combined with the Royal Infirmary, and that it should be placed in a separate building of the New Hospital.

*4th August* 1868.—The College met for the first time in their new Hall, the old one having been altered and enlarged.

Answers from the Queen and the Duke of Edinburgh to the Addresses presented to them were reported to the College.

Intimation was made that a marble bust, by Joseph, of the late Dr James Hamilton, senior, of Edinburgh, had been presented to the College by Dr George Bell. The thanks of the College were voted to Dr Bell.

The College resolved that in future all candidates for the Licence should be required to produce, prior to the final examination, a certificate of having studied Vaccination under a competent and recognised teacher.

*3d November* 1868.—A Licentiate of the College was deprived of his Licence for having circulated an indecent publication, and for having caused to be inserted in the newspapers advertisements of an unprofessional character.

*4th May* 1869.—A Honorarium of one hundred and fifty guineas was voted to Dr Samuel Somerville, Treasurer of the College, in recognition of his valuable services.

*1st February* 1870.—The College resolved that every candidate for the Licence should be required to pass an examination in Clinical Medicine, and agreed to a plan under which the examinations were to be carried out.

The College directed that a Supplemental Catalogue to the Library should be prepared and printed.

*22d February* 1870.—The College agreed to a Report by the Council of the College to the General Medical Council, as to the formation of a Joint Board for Medical Examination in Scotland.

*8th March* 1870.—The College agreed to a Report of the Council, on the Report on State Medicine, prepared by a Committee of the General Medical Council.

*31st May* 1870.—The College approved of the Report of the Medical Reform Committee on the Medical Act (1858) Amendment Bill.

*7th February* 1871.—The College subscribed fifty guineas to the local fund instituted to defray the expenses of the reception of the British Association for the Advancement of Science in Edinburgh in August next.

A portrait of the late Dr Begbie was presented to the College by his son, Dr James Warburton Begbie.

*2d May* 1871.—The College resolved to petition in favour of the Anatomy Act (1832) Amendment Bill, and the Habitual Drunkards' Bill.

The College agreed to procure a marble bust, by Brodie, of the late Sir James Young Simpson, Bart.

*6th February* 1872.—The College agreed to send Addresses of Congratulation to the Queen and Prince of Wales, on the recovery of the Prince from a severe attack of enteric fever.

Resolutions adopted at a Conference held at Glasgow, of Delegates from this College, the Royal College of Surgeons of Edinburgh, and the Faculty of Physicians and Surgeons of Glasgow, in reference to a remit from the General Medical Council as to the establishment of a Conjoint Examining Board for Scotland, were submitted to the College, and after discussion were approved of.

*7th May* 1872.—Answers to the Congratulatory Addresses to the Queen and Prince of Wales were reported to the College.

The Scheme for a Conjoint Board for Medical Examinations in Scotland, drawn up by the Scottish Branch of the General Council of Medical Education and Registration was laid before the College, and a Delegate was appointed to attend a Meeting of the Branch Council to express the opinion of the College on the Scheme.

*10th June* 1872.—The Delegate appointed at last meeting of the College to meet the Scottish Branch Council, laid the Scheme, as amended, before the College, to which the College gave its assent.

*6th May* 1873.—The College voted a sum of one thousand guineas in aid of a scheme for extending the scientific and educational buildings of the University of Edinburgh.

*5th August* 1873.—Read letter from Sir Alexander Grant, Principal of the University of Edinburgh, acknowledging with thanks on the part of the Senatus, the liberality of the College in voting a donation to the Building Scheme.

*4th November* 1873.—The thanks of the College were voted to Dr Alexander Wood, on his retirement from the office of Representative of the College at the General Medical Council, which he had held for fifteen years, for his able and valuable services.

*3d February* 1874.—The College agreed that Addresses of Congratulation be presented to her Majesty the Queen and his Royal Highness the Duke of Edinburgh, on the occasion of the marriage of the latter on the 23d of January.

*5th May* 1874.—Answers to the Congratulatory Addresses to the Queen and the Duke of Edinburgh were reported.

The College agreed that in future all candidates for the Licence of the College should be required to pass an examination in Surgery before the Examiners of the College, unless they had already done so before some other Qualifying Body.

The College voted a sum of one hundred guineas in aid of the Building Fund of the Royal Maternity Hospital.

The College voted the sum of twenty-five guineas as a subscription to the fund for erecting a statue to the late Dr David Livingstone, African explorer.

## Historical Sketch.

*29th December* 1874.—The College approved of a suggestion by the Chairman of the Board of Supervision, that in the interests of public health, members of the medical profession in Scotland be requested to make Returns to the Local Authority of all cases of infectious or contagious disease which may occur in their practice. At the same Meeting the College expressed its strong objection to a proposal by the Convener of the Public Health Committee of the Town Council of Edinburgh, that a clause should be introduced into the Public Health Act, rendering it compulsory on medical practitioners to report to the Local Authority all cases of infectious disease occurring in their practice.

*29th December* 1874.—The College resolved to establish a certificate of Qualification in State Medicine, and remitted to the Council to consider and report upon the details of the Examination which should be instituted.

The College voted the sum of three hundred guineas, to be expended in the purchase of a service of plate, to be presented to Dr D. R. Haldane on his retirement from the office of Secretary, which he had held for upwards of fifteen years.

The use of the Hall was granted to the President (Dr Lowe) for the purpose of giving an entertainment to the Fellows of the College.

*5th March* 1875.—The plate voted to Dr Haldane was presented to him at an Extraordinary Meeting of the College.

*4th May* 1875.—The College voted fifty guineas in aid of the Building Fund of the Livingstone Medical Missionary Memorial Dispensary.

The regulations proposed by the Council to be observed by candidates for the certificate in State Medicine were approved of by the College, and were adopted as temporary regulations.

The College voted a donation of ten guineas in aid of the funds of the Scottish Meteorological Society.

The Secretary stated that the President and Council of the College had had under consideration a Bill to amend the Medical Act 1858, so far as relates to the Registration of Women who have taken the Degree of Doctor of Medicine in a Foreign University, and that as the matter was urgent, they had petitioned against it. The diligence of the Council in forwarding the petition was approved of by the College.

*8th June* 1875.—The College agreed to entertain the Members of the British Medical Association at their approaching visit to Edinburgh, the entertainment to consist of a promenade, with music and refreshments, in the Hall of the Museum of Science and Art.

*3d August* 1875.—Two Licentiates of the College whose names had been removed by the General Medical Council from the Medical Register, in consequence of having been connected with a conspiracy to defraud, were declared to be no longer Licentiates of the College, and the Registrar was instructed to delete their names from the College Register.

*28th December* 1875.—Plans for additional Library accommodation, involving a probable cost of £3300, were approved of by the College.

*2d May* 1876.—The recommendations of a Conference of Representatives of the Royal Colleges of Physicians and Surgeons of Edinburgh, and of the Faculty of Physicians and Surgeons of Glasgow, in regard to improvements in the examinations for their Diplomas, were approved of by the College.

It was decided that no Fellow resident upwards of ten miles from Edinburgh should be permitted to borrow books from the Library without the special permission of the Council.

The College agreed to petition against the Bill introduced into Parliament by Mr Cowper Temple to amend the Medical Act 1858, as far as relates to the Registration of Women who have taken the Degree of Doctor of Medicine in a Foreign University.

## Historical Sketch.

The Treasurer announced that Dr T. H. Pattison, a Fellow of the College, had assigned two policies of insurance on his life, amounting to £850, for founding a Bursary towards the education of a male medical student in Edinburgh, under the direction and nomination of the Council of the College. The College accepted the assignation, voted its thanks to Dr Pattison, and agreed that the Bursary be named the Pattison Bursary.

*1st August* 1876.—The fee for the Licence of the College was raised to £15, 15s.

*7th August* 1877.—Two persons who had been deprived of the Licence of the College in consequence of their names having been removed from the Medical Register, but which had since been reponed by the General Medical Council, were restored to their position as Licentiates of the College.

A donation of ten guineas was voted to the Scottish Meteorological Society.

*5th February* 1878.—The College agreed to a reply to be made to the General Medical Council on the subject of Preliminary Examination.

*29th March* 1878.—The College agreed to support a Bill introduced into Parliament by the Duke of Richmond and Gordon, entituled the Medical Act (1858) Amendment Bill.

*6th August* 1878.—A Licentiate of the College whose name had been removed by the General Medical Council from the Medical Register, in consequence of his having been convicted of feloniously using instruments to procure miscarriage, was declared to be no longer a Licentiate of the College, and the Registrar was instructed to delete his name from the College Register.

*24th December* 1878.—The College voted two hundred and fifty guineas in aid of the subscription for the relief of the sufferers by the failure of the City of Glasgow Bank.

A letter was read from the Rev. Sir W. G. Carmichael, Bart., requesting the College's acceptance of a marble bust, by Sir John Steell, of the late Dr J. W. Begbie. The College accepted the offer, and voted thanks to the donor.

*4th February* 1879.—The President reported that he and the Council, as representing the College, had by invitation attended the Special Services in St Giles Cathedral Church on 22d December last, on the occasion of the death of the Princess Alice of Hesse.

*College disapproved of Medical Act Amendment Bill*

*14th March* 1879.—The College having considered the Medical Act (1858) Amendment Bill introduced into the House of Lords by the President of the Council, concluded that it was not expedient that a Conjoint Board be established for each division of the United Kingdom, and that previous to legislation taking place, the whole subject of Medical Reform should be submitted to a Select Committee of Parliament, and instructed the Council to take such steps as they might consider necessary to carry out the wishes of the College.

*College agreed to furnish two Wards in new Royal Infirmary*

*3d May* 1879.—The College agreed to contribute a sufficient sum to furnish two Medical Wards in the new Royal Infirmary. (The sum required amounted to £630.)

The Council reported that in accordance with the instructions of the College, they had forwarded a petition against the Medical Acts Amendment Bill to both Houses of Parliament.

*Select Committee of House of Commons on Medical Act Amendment Bill.*

*5th August* 1879.—It was reported to the College that the Medical Act Amendment Bill having passed the House of Lords and been introduced into the House of Commons, had been referred to a Select Committee, and that evidence to a certain extent had already been taken.

*Retiring allowance voted to late Officer.*

*16th December* 1879.—The College voted a retiring allowance of £75 per annum to their late Officer.

*College approved of proposal to hold next Meeting of International Medical Congress in London*

A communication was made from the Presidents of the Royal Colleges of Physicians and Surgeons of London, intimating that it was proposed to hold the next meeting of the International Medical Congress in London in 1881, and requesting to be informed how far the holding of the proposed Congress would meet with the approval and co-operation of this College. The College approved of the proposal, and gave power to the Council to send a Delegate to be present at a Preliminary Meeting, which it was proposed to hold.

## Historical Sketch.

*24th February* 1880.—A Committee was appointed to consider the Laws relative to admission to the Membership and Fellowship of the College, and to report at the next Quarterly Meeting of the College.

The College, by a majority, voted the sum of one hundred guineas towards the fund for the Restoration of St Giles Cathedral.

*3d May* 1880.—The Committee appointed to consider the Laws relative to admission to the Membership and Fellowship of the College, laid a Report before the College, which was approved of, and read for a first time.

*3d August* 1880.—Farther consideration of the Report as to the Laws relative to admission to the Membership and Fellowship of the College was postponed till the November Quarterly Meeting.

The College voted the sum of fifty guineas in aid of the fund required to meet the expenses consequent on the Meeting of the Congress of the National Association for the promotion of Social Science, to be held in Edinburgh in October next.

*2d November* 1880.—The Report of the Committee on the Laws relative to admission to the Membership and Fellowship of the College was approved of, and read for a second time.

The Treasurer reported that, under authority of the Council, he had on behalf of the College subscribed and paid five guineas towards defraying the expenses of the Library Association of the United Kingdom, which had met in Edinburgh last month. The College approved of, and ratified and confirmed the subscription made.

*1st February* 1881.—The Report of the Committee on the Laws relative to admission to the Membership and Fellowship of the College, which had been somewhat modified, was approved of, and read for a third time, and the Laws proposed in the Report were declared to be the Laws of the College.

*2d August* 1881.—The College voted that a sum of fifty pounds be paid annually, during the pleasure of the College, to the Clinical Tutor attached to the Wards of the Ordinary Physicians to the Royal Infirmary.

*£50 voted to aid in defraying expenses of International Medical Congress.*

The College voted that a sum of fifty pounds be paid towards defraying the expenses of the Meeting of the International Medical Congress to be held in London this month.

The Council reported to the College certain queries addressed by the Medical Acts Commission to the several Licensing Bodies, and submitted the reply which they proposed to make on behalf of the College. The College approved of the reply, and authorised the same to be transmitted as the reply of the College.

*Celebration of Bicentenary of Incorporation of the College.*

*7th February* 1882.—The Vice-President, in the absence of the President, reported that the Bicentenary of the Incorporation of the College had been celebrated at the Annual Dinner, held on 8th December last, which was attended by not only most of the Resident Fellows of the College, but also by Representatives of both Houses of Parliament, Her Majesty's Navy and Army, the Magistracy of Edinburgh, the College of Justice, and other eminent citizens, and by Representatives of the Medical Profession from Glasgow, and other Cities and Towns in Scotland.

# LAWS.

## CHAPTER I.

### Of the College and Common Seal.

1. THE College shall consist of Fellows and Members.  *The College.*

2. The business of the College shall be managed by the Fellows.  *College business to be managed by the Fellows.*

3. The Seal whereof the above is an engraving, is the Seal of this College; and shall be affixed to all Testimonials, Licences, Certificates, and other Public Acts of the College.  *The Common Seal.*

*To be kept by Secretary.*

4. The Common Seal shall be kept in the custody of the Secretary, and shall be affixed by him to such Documents as the College, Council, or President, shall direct.

*College shall grant Licences.*

5. The College shall grant Licences to practise Medicine and Midwifery, the holders of which shall be entitled Licentiates of the College. (See Chapter IV.)

---

## CHAPTER II.

### Of Fellows.

*Powers of the Fellows.*

1. The Fellows of the College alone shall be entrusted with the administration of the property and internal affairs of the College, and also with the enactment of its Laws, the election of its Fellows and its Members, the admission of its Licentiates, and the election of the President and Council.

*Who are eligible.*

2. No one shall be elected a Fellow of the College until he has been at least one year a Member thereof, and has attained the age of twenty-five years.

*How election made of each.*

3. Every motion for the election of a Fellow shall be made at a Quarterly Meeting of Fellows by one of the Fellows present, and seconded by another; and this motion shall be determined by ballot at the next Quarterly Meeting of Fellows,—a majority of three-fourths being necessary to carry it in the affirmative.

*Candidates announced to Fellows.*

4. The names and addresses of Candidates for admission as Fellows, with the names of their proposers and seconders, shall be announced by Billet to the Fellows on the Roll of Attendance, within one week from

the date of the Meeting at which the motion for their election has been made. The names and addresses here referred to shall be repeated in the Billet (Chapter IX., Law 9) summoning the Meeting at which the motion for election is to be determined.

5. If an urgent reason, satisfactory to the Council be assigned, a Candidate may be proposed at an Extraordinary Meeting of the Fellows summoned for the purpose, and his petition may be balloted for at an Extraordinary Meeting of the Fellows specially summoned for the purpose; provided that the holding of this Special Meeting be agreed to by a majority of five-sixths of the Fellows present at the Meeting at which the Candidate was proposed; provided also that not less than one week intervene between the two Meetings, and that due notice of the intended ballot be given in the Billets summoning the second Meeting. The Candidate shall in this case pay to the Treasurer a sum of ten guineas in addition to the ordinary Fees. *Election in cases of urgency.*

6. No Fellow shall take his seat in the College until the next Quarterly Meeting after his election,—intimation to attend being sent to him by the Clerk. *Taking of seat.*

7. The Fellows shall be placed on the Roll according to the date of their admission; and, when two or more Fellows are admitted on the same day, they shall be entered on the Roll according to the date of their diplomas; and if their diplomas be of the same date, they shall be enrolled according to seniority. *Order on Roll.*

8. Every Fellow resident within five miles from the General Post Office of Edinburgh shall, on his election, have his name placed on the Roll of Attendance, and shall pay the annual contribution, and be subject to all the Laws of the College regarding fines. Fellows resident beyond five miles shall have the option of *Roll of Attendance.*

having their names on the Roll of Attendance or not; but if their names be on the Roll of Attendance, they shall pay the Annual Contribution, and be subject to fines.

*Removal of names from Roll.*

9. Any Fellow may petition that his name be taken off the Roll of Attendance; which petition shall be determined by ballot at next Quarterly Meeting.

*Placing of name on Roll of Attendance.*

10. Any Fellow whose name is not on the Roll of Attendance may have it inserted by giving notice to the Secretary, who shall report to the next Quarterly Meeting; after which, the Fellow shall be entitled to all the privileges of the Fellowship, and may take his seat at the first Meeting of the College.

*Fellows leaving Edinburgh may have their names taken off the Roll.*

11. Any Fellow leaving Edinburgh for a length of time, and omitting to petition to have his name taken off the Roll of Attendance, or wishing the same to be continued on it during his absence, shall be charged with his Annual Contribution and fines.

*Fellows not on Roll not to have use of Library;*

12. Fellows whose names are not on the Roll of Attendance, shall not have the use of the Library and Reading-room, except in the cases specified in Laws 13 and 14.

*except with consent of Council.*

13. Fellows whose names are not on the Roll of Attendance, on coming to reside in Edinburgh, or within five miles thereof, for a period not exceeding six months, may, with consent of the Council, be allowed the use of the Library and Reading-room.

*Fellows not on Roll of Attendance may use Library.*

14. Fellows not on the Roll of Attendance, who reside permanently in Edinburgh, or within five miles thereof, but are not engaged in practice, may, with the consent of the Council, be allowed the use of the Library and Reading-room on payment of the Annual Contribution.

*Mode of reception of new Fellows.*

15. Each Fellow, on first taking his seat, shall be introduced by the Secretary to the President and

## Laws.

Fellows, who shall receive him standing. After the promissory obligation (Appendix No. I.) has been read aloud to him by the Secretary or Clerk (the President and Fellows still standing), he shall affix his name to it in the presence of the College, and he shall then receive the right hand of Fellowship from the President and Fellows present.

16. Petitions for admission as Fellows shall be in the form given in the Appendix No. II. The further proceedings upon such petitions shall be in the form prescribed in Laws 3 and 4 of this section. *Form of Petition.*

17. The Diploma presented by the College to its Ordinary Fellows shall be in the terms given in Appendix No. IV. *Form of Diploma.*

## CHAPTER III.

### Of Members.

1. Any Licentiate of a College of Physicians, or Graduate in Medicine of a British or Irish University, may be admitted a Member of the College, provided he has attained the age of twenty-four years, produced satisfactory testimonials as to his professional and social status, and satisfied the College as to his proficiency in Medical Science. *Who are eligible.*

2. The Council shall, at the Annual Meeting of the College for the election of Office-Bearers, appoint a Board of Examiners to conduct the Examination of Candidates. *Board of Examiners.*

3. Every Candidate for the Membership (except such as shall be admissible under the provisions of section 7) shall be examined—

*Subjects of Examination.*

(1.) On the Principles and Practice of Medicine, including Therapeutics.

(2.) Also on one of the following subjects, to be selected by the Candidate :—

(*a*) Pathology, including Morbid Anatomy ;
(*b*) Medical Jurisprudence and Public Health ;
(*c*) Midwifery and the Diseases of Women ;
(*d*) Psychological Medicine.

*Council to prepare Plan of Examination.*

4. The Council shall annually, at the Quarterly Meeting of the College in August, submit to the College the Plan of Examination for the Membership, and the dates at which it is proposed that the Examinations shall be held.

*Mode of Application.*

5. Application for the Membership shall be made through the Secretary, who shall transmit to the Candidate a copy of the Regulations and Plan of Examination, together with a Petition in terms of the Form in the Appendix No. III.

6. The Candidate shall return the Petition duly filled up to the Secretary, and shall at the same time transmit testimonials of recent date from well-known members of the profession, certifying as to his professional and social standing. These documents shall be submitted to the Council, who shall also employ such other methods of scrutiny as they may deem necessary. If satisfied as to the eligibility of the Candidate, the Council shall authorize his Examination by the Board of Examiners, who shall report the result of the Examination to the Council. If the report of the Examiners be satisfactory, the Council shall report the

*Must produce testimonials.*

same to the College at the next Quarterly Meeting, when it shall be competent for a motion to be made for the election of such Candidate to the Membership of the College.

7. If any Candidate who has attained the age of forty years, and has been a Registered Practitioner for not less than ten years, shall produce Testimonials showing that he has been distinguished for his scientific attainments, or eminence as a Medical Practitioner, the Council may, if they see fit, exempt him from the whole or any part of the prescribed Examination. *Certain Applicants to be exempted from Examination in whole or part.*

8. Every motion for the election of a Member shall be made at a Quarterly Meeting of the College by one of the Fellows present, and seconded by another, and the motion shall be determined by ballot at the next Quarterly Meeting; a majority of three-fourths of the Fellows present being necessary to carry it in the affirmative. *Mode of election.*

9. The names and addresses of Candidates, along with the names of their proposers and seconders, shall be announced by Billet to the Fellows on the Roll of Attendance, within one week from the date of the Meeting at which the motion for election has been made. The names and addresses here referred to shall be repeated in the Billet summoning the Meeting at which the motion for election is to be determined. *Names of Candidates to be announced to Fellows.*

10. The Members shall be placed on the Roll of Members according to the date of their Diplomas of Membership; and when two or more Members are admitted on the same day, they shall be enrolled according to professional seniority. *Order on Roll.*

11. The Diploma presented by the College to its Members shall be in terms of the Form given in the Appendix No. V. *Form of Diploma.*

## CHAPTER IV.

### Of Licentiates.

*Mode of application.*

1. Application for the Licence to practise Medicine shall be made through the Registrar, or, in the case of the Double Qualification, through the Inspector of Certificates.

*Who are eligible.*

2. Every Applicant, before receiving the Licence of the College, shall satisfy the Council that he is twenty-one years of age, that he is of good moral character, that he is not under articles of apprenticeship, and that he has fulfilled all the requirements that were in force at the date when he commenced his Medical studies.

*Council to prepare Curriculum of Study.*

3. The Council of the College shall annually, at the Quarterly Meeting in August, submit to the College the Curriculum of Study, and Plan of Examination for the Licence of the College.

*Copies of Curriculum to be printed.*

4. Copies of the existing Curriculum and Plan of Examination shall be printed and furnished to all applicants for the Licence.

*Certain Applicants to undergo a modified examination.*

5. Licentiates of the Royal College of Physicians of London, or of the King's and Queen's College of Physicians in Ireland; Graduates in Medicine of British and Irish Universities; Licentiates in Surgery of one of the Royal College of Surgeons, or of the Faculty of Physicians and Surgeons of Glasgow, or Licentiates of an Apothecaries' Company, will be required to undergo Examination in the following subjects only:—Practice of Medicine and Clinical Medicine, Materia Medica, Midwifery, and Medical Jurisprudence.

6. The Licence of the College may also be obtained in conjunction with that of the Royal College of Surgeons of Edinburgh, or of the Faculty of Physicians and Surgeons of Glasgow, under Regulations to be from time to time arranged between the College and these Bodies.

<small>Double Qualification.</small>

## CHAPTER V.

### Of the Fees.

1. The Fee to be paid by a Licentiate shall be fifteen guineas. <small>Fee of Licentiate.</small>

2. The Fee to be paid by a Member shall be thirty guineas. <small>Fee of Members.</small>

3. When a Member shall be raised to the rank of Fellow, he shall pay thirty guineas, exclusive of Stamp-duty. <small>Fee when a Member becomes a Fellow.</small>

4. When a Licentiate shall be raised to the rank of Member, he shall pay fifteen guineas. <small>Fee when a Licentiate becomes a Member.</small>

5. All Applicants for Licences, and all Candidates or Fellowship or Membership, must lodge their Fees, and the amount of Stamp-duty payable at the time to Government, with the Treasurer, previously to presenting their petitions, or appearing for Examination. <small>Fees to be lodged with Treasurer before petitions presented.</small>

## CHAPTER VI.

### Of Forfeiture of Fellowships, Memberships, and Licences.

*Keeping a public shop involves forfeiture of Fellowship or Membership.*

1. Any Fellow or Member of the College who shall by himself, copartners, or servants, keep a public Apothecary's, Druggist's, or Chemist's shop, shall, *ipso facto*, forfeit all the rights and privileges which he does or may enjoy as a Fellow or Member of the College, and his name shall be expunged from the List.

*Removal from the Register involves forfeiture of Fellowship, etc.*

2. Any Fellow, Member, or Licentiate of the College who shall, in accordance with the provisions of the Medical Act, Section XXIX., have his name removed from the Medical Register, shall be deprived, *ipso facto*, of his Fellowship, Membership, or Licence to practise, as given by the College.

*Unbecoming conduct involves forfeiture of Fellowship, etc.*

3. Any Fellow, Member, or Licentiate who, in the opinion of the College, shall have been guilty of conduct unbecoming the character of a Physician, may be deprived of all the rights and privileges which, as Fellow, Member, or Licentiate, he does or may enjoy.

*Censure or suspension.*

4. Any Fellow, Member, or Licentiate who shall, after due inquiry, be judged by the Fellows to have acted in an unbecoming or unprofessional manner, may be censured, or may be deprived for such time as the Fellows may determine, of all the rights and privileges which, as Fellow, Member, or Licentiate, he does or may enjoy.

*Mode of depriving of the Fellowship, etc.*

5. The proceedings for censure, suspension, or expulsion shall be as follow:—The motion for the censure,

suspension, or expulsion of the Fellow, Member, or Licentiate, shall contain a statement of the offence of which the Fellow, Member, or Licentiate is accused. This motion shall be submitted to the Council, and shall be laid by them, with their opinion thereon, before a Meeting of the Fellows, at which it shall be proposed and seconded. A vote of the Fellows shall then be taken, as to whether it is expedient to entertain the motion; and in the event of it being decided by a Majority that the motion shall be entertained, the farther proceedings shall be as follow:—The motion shall be determined at another Meeting of the Fellows, summoned at an interval of not less than three months after the first. The object of both these Meetings shall be announced in the Billets summoning the Meetings; and the Billets shall be issued one week previous to each Meeting. A Majority of three-fourths of those present shall be required to carry the motion.

6. The Clerk shall, within three clear days after the Meeting at which the motion has been proposed, transmit a copy of it to the Fellow, Member, or Licentiate accused. It shall be held sufficient evidence of this Law having been complied with, if the notice has been posted, with the address of the Fellow, Member, or Licentiate, as given in the College books, or in the latest issue of the Medical Register. *Clerk to send notice to Fellow, etc., accused.*

7. The Fellow, Member, or Licentiate accused, may appear and plead by himself, or by his Representative, at the Meeting at which the motion is to be considered. *The accused to appear by himself or Representative.*

8. It shall be in the power of the Council to shorten the period of three months between the tabling and discussion of the motion, should the Fellow, Member, or Licentiate accused, petition to that effect. *Council may shorten period of three months.*

## CHAPTER VII.

### On the Election of Office-Bearers.

*Election of President.*

1. At the Annual Meeting for the election of Office-Bearers (*vide* Chapter IX., Law 1), it shall be competent for any Fellow to propose one of the Fellows present, as President; and on his motion being seconded by another Fellow, the Fellow so nominated shall be elected President, if no other name be proposed. If, however, another name or names be duly proposed and seconded, a vote shall be taken, and the Fellow having the greatest number of votes shall be President of the College for the ensuing year.

*Nomination of Vice-President.*

2. The newly-elected President shall take the Chair, and nominate a Vice-President.

*Election of the other Members of Council.*

3. The President shall then nominate three of the Fellows present, not being in the Council, as Scrutineers. Thereupon the roll of the Fellows shall be called by the Clerk. Each Fellow present, as his name is called, shall then place on the table before the President a paper signed with his name, containing the names of six Fellows other than the President, chosen from among the Fellows then and there present, whom the Fellows voting may desire to elect to be, with the President, the Council of the College for the ensuing year. The Scrutineers shall, without leaving the room, arrange these Lists, and report to the College what names have received the greatest number of votes. Should any List be found incorrect, it shall be returned for correction, to the Fellow who signed it.

4. The Council of the College, who shall be Electors of the other Office-Bearers, shall immediately retire to another room, and shall there make choice of a Treasurer, a Secretary, a Registrar of Licentiates, a Curator of Museum, and a Librarian, all of whom must be Fellows of the College; and the Council shall further make choice of Examiners, a Clerk, an Auditor, an Under-Librarian, and an Officer. These Office-Bearers shall continue in office for one year. *Council to choose Office-Bearers.*

5. When the Electors return, the Clerk shall announce the names of the Office-Bearers. *Announcement of Office-Bearers.*

6. The same Fellow may be elected President for two years successively, but not for any longer consecutive period, unless by the consent of three-fourths of the Fellows present. But the same Fellow may be re-elected after having been out of office for two years. *President not to hold office for more than two years consecutively.*

7. In the event of the outgoing President having a majority of votes, but not a sufficient number to entitle him to re-election, the Fellow having the next highest number of votes shall not be declared President, but a new nomination (from which the retiring President shall be excluded) shall be made, and a new vote be taken, and the Fellow having the greatest number of votes shall de declared President for the ensuing year. *If retiring President have not enough of votes, another election necessary.*

8. The other Office-Bearers may be re-elected for an unlimited number of years. *No restriction on other Office-Bearers.*

9. In the event of a vacancy occurring in the office of a Councillor, an Examiner, or any other Office-Bearer, with the exception of the President, during the currency of the year, the Council shall have power to fill up the vacancy, such appointment to continue in force until the next Election-Meeting. *Council to have power to fill up vacancies.*

## CHAPTER VIII.

### Of the Powers and Duties of the Office-Bearers.

#### § 1. THE PRESIDENT.

*To be addressed by the Speakers.*
1. The President shall be addressed by those who speak in the Meetings.

*To regulate the debates.*
2. He shall keep order, regulate the debates, call the votes when necessary, and declare in what manner the question is determined.

*To have an ordinary and casting vote.*
3. He shall have one vote as Fellow, and a casting vote in case of an equal division.

*Cannot originate or second a motion.*
4. He shall not originate or second any motion while acting as Chairman.

*To appoint Committees.*
5. He shall appoint all Committees, and shall be *ex officio* a member of every Committee.

*To sign Diplomas.*
6. He shall sign all Diplomas issued by the College.

#### § 2. OF COMMITTEES.

*To be restricted as to time.*
1. At the appointment of every Committee (except standing Committees), a time shall be fixed for the business being finished which the College entrusts to it.

*Not to incur expense without a special vote of the College.*
2. No expenses shall be incurred by Committees without a special vote of the College, and a limitation of the sum to be expended.

*When to report.*
3. Committees appointed at one Quarterly Meeting shall bring up written Reports to the next Quarterly Meeting, unless it has been otherwise determined.

## § 3. The Treasurer.

1. The Treasurer shall receive, disburse, and be accountable for the Funds of the College.

2. He may pay, without any special order, the ordinary expenses of the College, but shall not pay or disburse any other sum without previous direction to that effect from the Council.

3. He shall balance his accounts every year on the 20th day of January, or, if that day shall happen to be Sunday, on the 19th January, and shall deliver, or cause to be delivered, to the Quarterly Meeting in February, the Auditor's Abstract and Statement of Accounts, containing his Charge and Discharge of the money belonging to the College, with a true state of his Accounts.

4. He shall keep a regular Book of Accounts, containing the various items of Income and Expenditure for the year, which Book shall be produced yearly at the February Meeting.

5. He shall keep a Book containing a statement of the Capital Account, which Book shall also be produced yearly at the February Meeting.

6. He may retain £20 in his hands; but any surplus above that shall be lodged in the Banking-house where the cash account of the College is kept; and when the funds so lodged shall exceed £500, as ascertained at the next Meeting of the Trustees of the College, such sum shall be placed on deposit receipt, in name of the Trustees, till an available security is found.

7. If at any time he shall have occasion to overdraw the cash account of the College, he shall on no account do so without the direct authority of the Council.

8. He may expend the sum of £5 on such repairs on the buildings as may be necessary; but when the expense exceeds that sum, he shall previously obtain the authority of the Council.

*Latitude as to repairs.*

9. All papers and vouchers relating to the property of the College, shall be lodged by the Treasurer in the Safe of the College, and the key retained by him.

*Vouchers to be lodged in Safe.*

10. After the Treasurer's accounts have been approved of, he shall see that the Report be regularly transcribed by the Clerk into the Minute-Book of the College.

*Report of accounts to be entered in Minutes.*

11. He shall, previously to the last Meeting of Council before the Quarterly Meeting in November of each year, give to the Clerk a list of the Trustees who may have been absent from any of the Meetings, in order that the penalties exigible from them may be collected and included in the Annual Statement of the contributions and fines.

*To keep a List of Trustees absent from the Meetings.*

12. On the resignation or retirement of the Treasurer, his books and relative vouchers shall be examined by a Committee appointed for the purpose, and if found correct, he shall be exonerated from his intromissions with the funds of the College. He shall also hand over all documents and papers in his custody, with a proper inventory thereof, to his successor in office, whose receipt for the same shall free him from all further responsibility regarding them.

*Proceedings consequent on a change of Treasurer.*

## § 4. THE AUDITOR.

1. The Auditor, who shall be a Chartered Accountant, shall examine the Treasurer's Annual Accounts, and frame an Abstract thereof, to be printed and submitted to the College at the Quarterly Meeting in February.

*To examine and report on Treasurer's Account.*

# Laws.

2. He shall also prepare a Statement of the funds and property of the College, to be printed and circulated with the Abstract. *To report on state of funds.*

3. For these services he shall receive such Fee as the Council may from time to time fix. *Salary.*

## § 5. THE TRUSTEES.

1. The Trustees shall consist of the Treasurer, and four Fellows to be selected by the Council, subject to the approval of the College. *How appointed.*

2. They shall invest all property belonging to the College, with the exception of the amount allowed to be retained in the Bank and in the Treasurer's hands (see Chap. VIII., Sect. 3, Law 6), in the name of the College, in its corporate capacity. *All property to be vested in name of the College.*

3. They shall hold two stated Meetings in the year, viz. :—on the second Tuesday of May and November, and shall also meet at such other times as the duties imposed upon them in regard to the property of the College (Chap XIII., Laws 3 to 5) may require. *Stated and occasional Meetings.*

4. On a vacancy occurring in the office of Trustee by death, resignation, or otherwise, the Council shall, within a month, nominate a successor, subject to the approval of the College at its next Meeting. *Vacancies how to be filled up.*

## § 6. THE EXAMINERS.

1. The Council shall choose from time to time Examiners in Preliminary Education, according to the subjects professed by the Applicants. *The Examiners in Preliminary Education.*

2. Should the Examiners in Preliminary Education not be Fellows of the College, the President or Vice-President, or one, at least, of the Examiners of the *Some Fellow of College to be present at Preliminary Examination.*

College; or, failing them, some Fellow of the College appointed by the Council shall be present at the Examination.

3. The Examiners of the College, annually chosen at the Election Meeting, or who may be appointed by the Council to fill the vacancies which may occur between the Election Meetings, shall conduct the Professional Examination of Applicants.

4. The Examiners shall have power to conduct the Examinations at such times and places as they may select, and to adjourn them as often as may seem advisable.

### § 7. THE SECRETARY.

1. The Secretary shall take charge of all the correspondence of the College, and cause copies of all his important letters to be entered by the Clerk, or otherwise, in the Letter-Book of the College.

2. He shall, at all Meetings of the College or Council, take himself, or cause to be taken by the Clerk, Minutes of the Proceedings, and shall see that they are properly extended, and, after approval, engrossed in the respective Minute-Books.

3. He shall submit to the College the Opinion of the Council on all motions or other business which has been considered by them, and shall give such explanations to the College as the Council may direct.

4. He shall, in conjunction with the President, sign all Diplomas issued by the College.

5. He shall keep under his custody the copper-plates on which are engraved the forms of Diplomas for Fellows, Members, and Licentiates, and also the lithographed or printed forms of Petition for the Fellowship and Membership.

## Laws.

6. He shall keep under his custody, in the Safe of the College, the various Minute-Books, Letters, and Papers belonging to the College. The Current Letter-Book and Minutes of Council he may keep in his own house, but the Minute-Book of the College is, on no account whatever, to be removed from the building.

7. He shall allow access to these Minutes at all times to the Fellows of the College; but it shall be in the power of the Council to authorize the Secretary to withhold the Minutes of the Council as to any particular business still in dependence.—Other parties shall only be permitted to inspect them on making written application to the Council and receiving its sanction.

8. He shall direct the Clerk to summon Meetings of the College and Council, and shall furnish him with a list of the business to be transacted at each Meeting, in order that it may be duly entered in the Billets by which the Meeting is called. He shall also, previously to each Quarterly or Extraordinary Meeting of the College, cause a programme of the business to be suspended in the Reading-Room.

9. He shall, previously to the Meeting of Council before the Quarterly Meeting of the College in November of each year, give to the Clerk a list of Members of the Council who may have been absent at any of the Meetings, in order that the fines exigible from them may be collected and included in the Annual Statement of the contributions and fines.

### § 8. REGISTRAR.

1. The Council shall annually, at the Election Meeting, nominate one of the Fellows of the College to be the *Registrar* for the ensuing year.

*Duties of Registrar.*

2. The Registrar shall have charge of the whole correspondence regarding applications for the Licence of the College.

3. The Registrar shall arrange in regard to Applicants coming before the several Boards of Examination.

*May also be Secretary.*

4. The same Fellow may hold the office of Secretary and Registrar.

*Remuneration.*

5. The Registrar shall receive for his services such salary as the Council may from time to time determine.

## § 9. THE LIBRARIAN.

*To have control of Library*

1. The Librarian shall have the general control of the Library, and superintend the ordering of Books, and the performance of the duties of the Library by the Under-Librarian and Officer.

*To Register absentees from Library Committee.*

2. He shall, previously to the Meeting of Council before the Quarterly Meeting of the College in November of each year, give to the Clerk a list of Members of the Library Committee who may have been absent from any of the Meetings of the Committee, and also of those Fellows who may have committed any breach of the Regulations of the Library, in order that the fines exigible from them may be collected and included in the Annual Statement of the contributions and fines.

## § 10. UNDER-LIBRARIAN.

*Hours of attendance.*

1. The Under-Librarian shall attend at least one stated hour daily, from 4 to 5 o'clock P.M., for giving out and receiving Books, and performing all other duties devolving on him under the Regulations for the Library.

2. He shall regularly enter all Books, purchased or presented to the College, in the Library Journal kept for that purpose, and in the Alphabetical Catalogue. *(Registers to be kept.)*

3. He shall receive and execute the instructions of the Librarian and Library Committee regarding the concerns of the Library; and shall also attend Meetings of the Library Committee when required. *(To execute instructions of Librarian.)*

### § 11. THE CLERK.

1. The Clerk shall attend all the Meetings of the College, the Quarterly Meetings of the Council, and any other Meetings of the Council, or of any of the Committees at which his assistance may be required. *(To attend Meeting of College or Council.)*

2. In the event of the Clerk being unavoidably prevented from attending a Meeting, some competent person deputed by him may attend in his place. But the Clerk shall in no case be absent without such properly qualified substitute, for whom he shall be considered responsible; and he shall in each case furnish a sufficient excuse to the College for his own absence. *(When absent, shall provide a substitute.)*

3. He shall call the Roll at the commencement and close of each Meeting of the College, and register the fines against those who are late, or absent. *(To call Roll.)*

4. He shall read the Minutes of the College, and any Petitions of Candidates for admission as Fellows or Members. *(To read Minutes and Petitions.)*

5. He shall, at each Meeting of the College, minute the proceedings, and shall subsequently extend them under the direction of the Secretary. *(To keep Minutes.)*

6. He shall submit the draft of the Minute so prepared to the Quarterly Meeting of Council previously to its being read at the next Quarterly Meeting of the *(To submit Minutes to Council.)*

College. He shall, within four days after each Minute has received the sanction of the College, cause it to be engrossed in the Minute-Book.

7. He shall, when directed by the Secretary, copy all letters or other documents which the interests of the College may require.

8. He shall, on or before the Quarterly Meeting in November, annually collect all the fines incurred by Fellows, and shall keep a regular statement of them and of the contributions, which he shall annually submit to the Auditor of the Accounts.

9. He shall engross all Financial Statements that have been approved of by the College, in the Account and Minute-Book of the College.

10. He shall issue the Billets summoning the Meetings of the College, with such list of the business to be transacted as shall be furnished him by the Secretary.

11. He shall intimate to every Fellow on the Roll of Attendance, the names of Candidates for the Fellowship and Membership, within one week after the Meeting at which the motion for their election has been made.

12. He shall intimate to Fellows and Members their election, and to Fellows the time when they are expected to take their seats in the College.

13. He shall, within three days of the proposal of any motion, for the censure, suspension, or expulsion of a Fellow, Member, or Licentiate, transmit a copy of the motion to the Fellow, Member, or Licentiate accused.

14. He shall, before the 31st of January of each year, arrange the papers and vouchers of the College for the past year, and shall prepare an Index of the same, to be given to the Secretary for custody.

15. For these services he shall receive an annual salary of £25 sterling; and a further sum of two guineas for attendance at and engrossing the Minutes of each Extraordinary Meeting at which his presence may be required. *Salary*

### § 12. THE OFFICER.

1. He shall be elected by the Council, and hold his office during their pleasure. *How to be chosen.*

2. He shall reside in the apartments provided for him in the College; and shall give his whole time to the performance of the business of the College. *To reside in College.*

3. He shall deliver Billets and other Papers of the College to their addresses in Edinburgh, and shall post those for Fellows at a distance, on his being instructed to do so by the President, Secretary, Clerk, or the Chairman of any Committee. *To deliver Billets and other Papers.*

4. He shall keep the Hall, and other apartments of the College, clean and in good order, and shall attend at the door at every Meeting. *To keep apartments in order.*

5. He shall be ready at all times to give out Books to Fellows on receipt, under the Regulations in Chap. XIV. *To give out Books.*

6. He shall have the apartments ready for the use of the Fellows every morning at 10 A.M. *To open College.*

7. He shall put out all lights, and see that the fires are properly extinguished, and the College shut every evening at 10 P.M. *To shut College.*

8. Besides coal, gas, and apartments, he shall receive such salary as the Council may appoint. *Salary.*

## CHAPTER IX.

### Of the Meetings of the College.

1. A Meeting of the Fellows of the College shall be held annually, at ten o'clock in the forenoon, on St Andrew's Day, if it shall happen to fall on a Thursday: and, if not, on the first Thursday thereafter,—for the sole purpose of electing Office-Bearers for the year ensuing.

2. There shall be held four Ordinary Quarterly Meetings,—viz., on the first Tuesday of February, May, August, and November,—at three o'clock in the afternoon.

3. On the Friday preceding each Quarterly Meeting, the Council shall meet in the Hall at such hour as they may from time to time determine, to consider the business which is to be brought before the Fellows on the Tuesday following, and to instruct the Secretary or Clerk what notices are to be circulated in the Billets, which shall be issued on the Friday evening.

4. The business of the College shall be managed solely by the Fellows, seven of whom shall be a quorum.

5. The President or Council may call Extraordinary Meetings of the Fellows, when deemed necessary; the business for these Meetings shall be arranged by the Council, and printed in the Billets summoning the Meeting.

6. The President shall be bound to call an Extraordinary Meeting of the Fellows, on a requisition to that effect, specifying the purpose of such Meeting, and signed

by any five of the Fellows, being delivered to him or to the Secretary of the College.

7. The President, Secretary, or Treasurer, may, severally, call a Meeting of the Council when they think it necessary.

8. Every Fellow of the College resident in Great Britain and Ireland, whose name is on the Roll of Attendance, shall be summoned to the Meetings of the College. The summons shall be by a Billet specifying the day and hour, and the business to be transacted at the Meeting.

9. The Billets summoning the Meetings, and generally, all intimations required by the Laws of the College, may be sent by post; and, in this case, the fact of such Biilets having been posted to the address in Great Britain or Ireland last furnished to the Clerk by any Fellow, shall be held to be sufficient evidence of legal delivery. The Billets for Fellows resident in Edinburgh, or in the Extended Royalty thereof, may be delivered by the officer; and in this case, proof of a Billet being delivered at the last address furnished to the Clerk shall be held to be sufficient evidence of legal delivery.

## CHAPTER X.

### Of the Order of Business.

#### § 1. OF ELECTION MEETINGS.

The business shall be transacted in the form prescribed in Chapter VII.

### § 2. OF THE QUARTERLY MEETINGS OF FELLOWS.

1. The Clerk shall read the Minutes of the last Quarterly Meeting, and of all subsequent Meetings of the Fellows. These Minutes, when approved of, shall be signed by the President, or by the Chairman for the time being.

2. Petitions of Candidates for admission as Fellows shall be considered.

3. Ballots for admission to the Fellowship shall take place.

4. Petitions of Candidates for admissions as Members shall be considered.

5. Ballots for admission to the Membership shall take place.

6. The names of those who have received the Licence of the College since the previous Quarterly Meeting shall be announced.

7. Reports of Committees shall be received and discussed.

8. Any other business previously proposed, according to the Laws, shall be brought forward by the Secretary. (*Vide* Chap. XI.)

### § 3. OF EXTRAORDINARY MEETINGS OF FELLOWS.

The order of business shall be the same as in Sec. 2, except that no Minutes shall be read, and that no business shall be transacted except that for which the Meeting has been specially summoned.

### § 4. FORMS APPLICABLE TO ALL MEETINGS.

1. All Meetings shall be constituted by the President taking the chair, at the hour appointed; and all Meet-

ings shall be dissolved or adjourned by the President leaving the chair.

2. In the event of the President being absent, the Vice-President shall take the chair; and in the absence of both, the chair shall be taken by the Fellow first on the Roll of Attendance who may be present. *Chairman in absence of President.*

3. At the commencement and close of all Meetings, the Clerk shall call the Roll of Attendance, and he shall fine those who are absent. *Roll-call.*

4. Notice of all business to be transacted at the Meetings of the College shall be circulated with the Billets; and in the case of Billets for the election of Fellows and Members, or for the forfeiture of Fellowships and Memberships, or in the case of motions affecting the Property and Laws of the College, the Billets must be issued at least one week before the day of Meeting, and must be otherwise in accordance with the Bye-Laws. *Notice of all business to be given in the Billets.*

## CHAPTER XI.

### Motions, Laws, and Protests.

1. No business can be taken up at any Meeting of the College, other than that specially provided for in the Laws, unless it has been first considered and reported on by the Council, or by a Committee appointed by the College for the purpose. *Business to be first submitted to the Council.*

2. All business shall be brought before the College, either in the form of a Report by the Council or a Committee, or of a motion by a Fellow of the College. *Form in which business shall be brought before the College.*

3. When business is to be brought before the College by a Report, it shall either be circulated with the Billets summoning the Meeting, or be laid on the Library table for the consideration of the Fellows, at least three clear days before the Meeting; and of this due notice shall be given in the Billets.

4. No Report, nor any recommendation contained in a Report, shall be approved, disapproved, or otherwise dealt with by the College, unless by a motion or amendment duly proposed and seconded.

5. When business is to be brought before the College by a motion, a copy thereof shall be sent to the Secretary at least four clear days before the Meeting of the College at which it is proposed to be discussed.

6. The Secretary shall submit any motion so received by him to a Meeting of the Council, to be held at least three clear days before the Meeting of the College at which the said motion is to be considered; and the Council shall report their opinion of the expediency of passing the motion to the said Meeting of the College.

7. The Secretary shall cause a copy of the proposed motion, or an abstract thereof, to be circulated with the Billets summoning the Meeting at which it is to be brought forward, and the motion itself to be suspended in that part of the College where notices are usually posted.

8. It shall be lawful for any Fellow, at any Meeting of the College, to move the approval or disapproval of any Report and of any recommendation contained in such Report, or to propose, either in the way of motion or amendment, any modification of any such recommendation; provided always that the Report has been circulated with the Billets summoning the Meeting at which it is to be considered, or that it has been laid

on the Library table at least three days before the Meeting, and that intimation has been made to the Fellows that it is so open for their inspection.

9. It shall not be lawful, however, under the foregoing Law, for any Fellow, while a Report is under consideration, to table any motion or amendment relating to matters not brought before the College in the Report.

10. All motions shall be determined by the votes of a majority, except in cases otherwise provided for in the Laws.

11. Motions for the abrogation or alteration of a Law shall be approved of by three several Meetings of the College before they are adopted, a vote being taken for or against at each Meeting. Should such a motion, however, at its first or second reading, be approved of by five-sixths of the Fellows present, it may be immediately adopted and acted on as a temporary regulation.

12. No Fellow shall speak oftener than once on a motion, except the mover, who shall have a right to reply, after which the debate shall be concluded.

13. Any Fellow present at a Meeting, may protest in his own name, and in the name of those present who may adhere to him, against any decision come to by the College. The reasons for such protest shall be assigned either at the time, or shall be given in at the next Meeting of the College.

14. It shall not be lawful to take any exception to the Minutes, except on the ground that their narrative of the *res gestæ* is inaccurate, or that the Meeting in question had not been properly summoned.

15. The College may reject any document, protest, or instrument, the language of which may be considered objectionable, until amended to the satisfaction of the College.

## CHAPTER XII.

### Of the Contributions and Fines.

*For absence at Election or Quarterly Meetings.*

1. Every Fellow who shall be absent during the Meeting for Election, or during any of the Quarterly Meetings, shall pay a fine of 2s. 6d.

*For absence at Extraordinary Meetings.*

2. Every Fellow who shall be absent during an Extraordinary Meeting shall be fined 1s.

*Fine for not answering to name.*

3. Every Fellow who shall not answer to his name when the Roll is called at the beginning or end of any Meeting, shall be fined 6d.

*Fine for leaving Meeting.*

4. Any Fellow leaving the room during any of the Statutory Meetings of the Fellows before the Chairman has declared the Meeting ended, shall be fined 1s.; if during an Extraordinary Meeting, 6d.

*Fine for absence of Clerk;*

5. If the Clerk be absent without an excuse satisfactory to the Fellows, and without sending a properly qualified substitute, he shall pay a fine of 5s.

*for absence from Council;*

6. At the Quarterly Meetings of Council, any Member of Council absent during the whole Meeting shall be fined 2s. 6d., and at all other Meetings of Council, 1s. Every Member of Council absent when the roll is called, at the beginning or end of the Council Meetings, shall be fined 6d.

*for absence from Library or Museum Committee;*

7. Members of Committee absent from a Meeting of the Library or Museum Committee shall be fined 1s. for every such absence.

*for absence from Meeting of Trustees;*

8. Trustees absent from a Meeting of Trustees shall be fined 2s. 6d. for every such absence.

9. No excuses shall be sustained for absence from the Meetings, excepting being confined to the house by sickness, or being absent from Scotland.

10. Each Fellow on the Roll of Attending Fellows shall pay annually, at the Quarterly Meeting held in November, one guinea of contribution, and such fines as he may have incurred.

11. The Clerk shall annually make up, and lay before the Quarterly Meeting of the Council previous to the Quarterly Meeting of the College in November, a list of the fines incurred by Fellows during the past year.

12. The gross amount of fines due by each Fellow shall be appended to the Billet summoning him to the Quarterly Meeting of the Fellows in November.

13. The Clerk shall be bound, on application, to show to any Fellow a list of the separate occasions on which he has been fined.

14. The Council shall meet within ten days after the November Meeting of the Fellows, for the purpose of considering appeals against fines; and no subsequent appeal can be entertained unless the Fellow appealing was not in Edinburgh at the time when the Meeting for hearing appeals was held.

15. All appeals shall be given in to the Clerk in writing, and signed by the appellant; and the Council shall have power to adjourn, if necessary, and to request the appellant to attend, for the purpose of giving such explanation as may be desired.

16. No appeal shall be received after the lapse of one year from the Quarterly Meeting of the College in November.

17. Any Fellow who may be in arrear of his annual contributions and fines for a longer period than two

years, shall, after due intimation having been giving twice to him, at the interval of a month, be deprived of the use of the Library and Reading-Room, and of the privilege of attending the Meetings of the College, and shall have his name struck off the Roll of Attendance. No Fellow who is in arrear of his contribution and fines for two years shall be allowed to vote at the election of Office-Bearers.

## CHAPTER XIII.

### Of the Property of the College.

1. No motion tending to alienate any part of the property of the College, or apply it to other than the ordinary purposes of the College, shall be discussed except at Extraordinary Meetings called for the purpose.

No such alienation shall take place unless approved of by a majority of three-fourths of the Fellows present, at three several Meetings, eight days at least intervening between each.

2. No sum of money shall be voted in donation, subscription, or otherwise, excepting for the ordinary expenses of the College, till the propriety thereof has been considered at two several Meetings, eight days at least intervening between each. One of these may be a Quarterly Meeting, provided intimation of the proposal has been given in the Billets; and there must be a majority of three-fourths of the Fellows who shall be

present at each of these two Meetings, to warrant such a proposal. But if the sum proposed do not exceed ten guineas sterling, it shall be competent for the Fellows, by a majority of three-fourths of the Fellows present, to vote such sum immediately at any Meeting, Quarterly or Extraordinary, provided in either case notice has been given in the Billets summoning the Meeting.

3. The securities for all the sums of money or property that may belong to, or constitute any part or portion of the funds of the College, and all heritable rights connected therewith, shall be conceived and taken to and in favour of the College in its corporate name, or in favour of the persons who may be Trustees for the time being, and to their successors in office.

4. The Trustees shall have power to lend out and invest the monies belonging to the College upon bonds, heritable or moveable, debenture bonds of any established Railway Company, in the purchase of Government Stock, Stock of the Bank of England, or on any security sanctioned by Act of Parliament or the Legal Courts of the country.

5. No purchase or sale of property or stock shall be made at any time by the said Trustees, without the special consent of four-fifths of the said Trustees, acting for the time being, expressed by a Minute entered in the sederunt-book of the Trustees, and subscribed by the Trustees so consenting and approving.

## CHAPTER XIV.

### Library and Library Committee.

*Committee of Committee.*

1. The President, Vice-President, Treasurer, and Librarian, together with two other Fellows appointed annually, at the Quarterly Meeting in August, shall form a Committee for the purchase of books and superintendence of the Library, and shall meet at least once a month.

*Books not to be lent.*

2. The attending Fellows of the College may borrow any books from the Library, excepting the ten volumes of MSS. given to the College by Sir John Pringle, and such other books as, from their value or other causes, the Library Committee think it inexpedient to circulate. A list of books not allowed to be lent shall be hung in the Library for the information of the Fellows.

*Receipts from Fellows.*

3. No book shall be lent out unless a receipt be given for it, or the Fellow may leave a signed list of the books he wishes to procure from the Library, which shall be held in place of a receipt. Fellows returning books must see that their receipts are cancelled, as otherwise they will be held responsible for any books lost that are entered in their names.

4. No Fellow resident beyond ten miles from Edinburgh shall be permitted to borrow Books from the Library except by special permission of the Council.

*Book duty of Sub-Librarian in Office.*

5. The Sub-Librarian shall attend daily at the hour appointed, for giving out and receiving books, and the performance of other duties connected with the Library.

In his absence, the presses shall be kept constantly locked; but the key shall be entrusted to the officer, who shall give out books to Fellows for consultation, he remaining in attendance at the Hall to receive and replace such books immediately when returned. The officer shall also give out books which are allowed to circulate among the Fellows, on taking a receipt for the same, which he shall hand over to the Sub-Librarian at his next visit, for insertion in the receipt-book.

6. The Sub-Librarian shall be responsible for all books lost which are entered in the receipt-book, and for which he can show no receipt; and the officer for all such as are neither entered in the book, nor acknowleged by the signature of any Fellow.

<small>Responsibilities of Sub-Librarian and Officer.</small>

7. Any books which have been less than a year in the Library, may be called in after being a fortnight, and all other books after being a month, in the possession of Fellows. Any Fellow neglecting to return a book after intimation to do so has been duly sent him by the Sub-Librarian, shall be fined one shilling for each day that he detains it, and no other book shall be lent to him in the meantime.

<small>Books may be called in, and fine for neglect.</small>

8. All books and periodicals shall (unless withheld by order of the Library Committee) lie on the table of the Library for a month after their reception. On being withdrawn from the table, the Sub-Librarian shall insert in the Library Catalogues their titles and places on the shelves; after which they shall be permitted to circulate among the Fellows. The numbers of periodicals, after being removed from the table, shall be laid aside until they form a volume, and then bound. In the meantime, they may be given out to Fellows under the ordinary regulations, but liable to be called in when wanted for binding.

<small>Not to be issued for a month after their receipt.</small>

9. A list shall be regularly kept by the Sub-Librarian of all books and periodicals laid upon the table, together with the date of their reception and removal. This list it shall be the duty of the officer to compare with the books actually on the table, every morning after 10 o'clock; reporting to the Sub-Librarian any that he finds missing, in order that they may be traced, and the proper penalty inflicted for their unauthorized removal or detention.

10. In the evenings, after 10 o'clock, the officer may give out to Fellows, to take home with them, any of the books or periodicals which are laid on the Library table; on condition of their being returned by 10 o'clock the next morning. He shall mark down in a proper book, their titles and the names of the Fellows to whom they are delivered, taking a receipt for the same; and if not returned at the time appointed, shall record against the offender a fine of one shilling for each hour they are detained.

11. Any Fellow removing books from the Hall without informing the Sub-Librarian or Officer, shall be fined five shillings for each offence. Newspapers shall on no account whatever be removed from the Reading-Room.

12. The Catalogues of the Library, with all recent additions inserted; the Library table book; the evening receipt book; the proposal book, and a list of fines incurred for infringing the regulations of the Library, shall be regularly laid before the Committee at each of their Meetings.

13. Fellows whose names have been taken off the Roll of Attendance may avail themselves of the privileges of the Library and Reading-room, under the regulations contained in Chap. II., Laws 13 and 14. Strangers wishing to consult books, if unattended by Fellows, must have the permission of the Council in each case, and shall do so in an adjoining apartment.

14. At the Quarterly Meeting in May every year, all books borrowed shall be ordered in within a week after that day, in order that the Librarian and Committee may institute an examination and comparison with the Press Catalogue of all the books in the Library; which they shall do within a fortnight after the said Quarterly Meeting. Fellows who neglect to comply with this order shall be fined one shilling for each book and each day of detention. The books shall be called in and examined in like manner on a vacancy in the offices of Sub-Librarian or Officer, before being handed over to the custody of a successor.

15. After such examination of the Library, a list of any books standing in the receipt book against any Fellow as unreturned, shall be sent to him, and he shall be fined six shillings per week for every book retained thereafter, unless he intimate that he has lost the book.

16. In every case where an intimation of loss has been made, and also in every case where a book has remained unreturned for three months after it has been recalled, the Librarian shall have power to purchase a copy of the missing book at the expense of the Fellow who has failed to return it.

17. The price paid for such book shall absolve the Fellow from all fines for its non-return, and shall be collected along with, and be subject to all the regulations regarding the fines of the College.

18. The Committee may from time to time make temporary regulations in regard to the Library. But such regulations shall not be acted on until approved of by the Council, and the whole or a part of them may be suspended or abolished by a vote of a majority of the Fellows at any Quarterly Meeting of the College.

Such temporary regulations, moreover, shall be held to be in force so long only as a copy of them hangs in a conspicuous part in the Reading-Room or Library.

## CHAPTER XV.

### Museum and Museum Committee.

*Constitution of Committee.*

1. The President, the Professor of Materia Medica in the University of Edinburgh (if a Fellow of the College), the Curator of the Museum, and two other Fellows appointed annually, at the Quarterly Meeting in August, shall form a Committee for the superintendence of the Museum, and shall meet as occasion requires.

*Curator to keep keys.*

2. The Curator shall keep the keys of the Museum cases, arrange the specimens according to a certain scientific order, and see that all the specimens are properly put up and preserved.

*Curator to enter donations.*

3. The Curator shall enter in a book kept for the purpose, a particular description of every article presented to the Museum of the College, with the name of the donor, and the date of its presentation, and shall exhibit to the College, at the first Quarterly Meeting thereafter, the donations received since its last Meeting.

*Specimens not to be handled.*

4. No specimen shall be handled or removed from the glass case, except in the presence of the Curator.

*Admission of visitors.*

5. Any Fellow of the College may give a written order for the admission of visitors to the Museum; but the cases shall not be opened to such visitors without

the consent of the Museum Committee previously obtained, and in the presence of the Curator or one of the Members of the Museum Committee appointed for this purpose.

6. The Curator shall, previously to the meeting before the Quarterly Meeting of the College in November in each year, give to the Clerk a list of those Members of the Museum Committee who may have been absent from any of the Meetings, in order that the fines exigible from them be collected and included in the Annual Statement of contributions and fines.

*Curator to register fines for absence from Museum Committee.*

## CHAPTER XVI.

### Of Diplomas, etc.

1. All the Diplomas of the College shall be engraved according to a form approved of by the Council. The plates shall be kept in the custody of the Secretary. Every Diploma issued by the College shall be signed by the President, and countersigned by the Secretary.

*Forms of Diplomas.*

2. Forms of petition for admission to the Fellowship and Membership shall be kept by the Secretary, and be furnished by him to intending Candidates.

*Forms of Petitions.*

## CHAPTER XVII.

### Certificates of Qualification to Lecture.

1. Any Fellow of the College desirous of being recognised as a Lecturer by the College and other Licensing Boards, shall make written application to the Secretary, who shall lay the same within ten days thereafter before the Council. The Council shall then appoint five well-qualified gentlemen to be a Board of Examiners; three of whom shall be a quorum.

2. The Board having met and determined on the mode of examination, shall inform the Candidate of the time and place where such examination shall be held. The examination shall consist of

   1. Questions to be answered either *viva voce* or in writing.
   2. A lecture on some part of the subject which the Candidate proposes to teach, in the course of which he shall give appropriate illustrations, manipulations, or demonstrations.
   3. He shall also give proof of possessing available means for illustrating the course.

3. In the event of the decision of the Board being favourable, the President shall confer a Certificate of Qualification to teach at the first Meeting of the College thereafter, or at an Extraordinary Meeting to be called for the purpose.

4. The Certificate of Qualification to Teach shall be in the form given in the Appendix No. VII.

## Laws.

5. For the examination of Lecturers not Fellows either of this College or of the College of Surgeons (which examination is to be conducted by a Joint Board of the two Colleges), the Council shall nominate an equal number of gentlemen with those appointed by the sister College.

6. Previously, however, to any such Applicant being taken on trial, a petition from him shall be presented to the President of either College, with a testimonial as to his general character, signed by at least three Fellows of either College.

7. The number composing the Joint Board shall be left to the decision of the Councils of the two Colleges.

8. The sum of ten guineas shall in each case be paid to the Board of Examiners, one-half by the Candidate, and the other half, in the case of his being a Fellow, out of the College funds. When one who is not a Fellow is examined, he shall pay the whole sum required.

# APPENDIX.

### No. I.

FORM OF PROMISSORY OBLIGATION to be signed by every FELLOW before taking his seat in the College.

I_____ , one of the Fellows of the Royal College of Physicians of Edinburgh, do, by subscribing these presents, solemnly declare and surely promise, *First*, That I shall all my life, according to my power, preserve and maintain the privileges, liberties, jurisdiction, and authority granted to the said College by her sacred Majesty's gracious Charter, dated 25th August, and sealed 31st October 1861, for the good and necessary ends and uses therein mentioned. *Secondly*, That I shall avail myself of all occasions to promote the welfare, prosperity, and utility of the said College, and shall always give my Vote, when it is asked, as I conscientiously think may be most conducive to these purposes. *Thirdly*, That I shall, as far as I am able, promote and preserve unity, concord, amity, and good order among all the Fellows, Members, Licentiates, and Candidates thereof; and shall heartily wish and endeavour to promote the prosperity of them all. *Fourthly*, That so long as I continue a Fellow of the said College, I shall at all times be subject to the due order and government of the College, according to the foresaid Charter, and shall conform and be obedient to the Laws and Regulations of the College, as the same are and shall be from time to time enacted. *Fifthly*, That I shall never divulge or publish anything that is acted or spoken, or proposed to be transacted, in any Meeting of the said College, or Council or Court thereof, without leave asked and obtained, according to the Laws prescribed by the College. All the aforesaid articles I hereby promise to observe, and never wittingly and willingly to break any one of them, as I desire to be held and respected an honest man.

No. II.

FORM OF PETITION for admission as FELLOWS.

*Unto the Much Honoured the* PRESIDENT *and Remanent* FELLOWS *of the Royal College of Physicians in Edinburgh.*

THE

PETITION of _____

HUMBLY SHEWETH,

THAT, for several years, I applied myself to the study of Medicine, and have obtained the Membership of the Royal College of Physicians of Edinburgh, conform to my Diploma, dated
and being willing to observe the whole Laws and Regulations of the College,

May it therefore please the Royal College to admit me as a Fellow of the College, with power to enjoy all rights, liberties, and privileges which any other Fellow does or may enjoy.

## No. III.

FORM OF PETITION for admission as MEMBERS.

*Unto the Much Honoured the* PRESIDENT *and* FELLOWS *of the Royal College of Physicians of Edinburgh.*

THE

PETITION of ─────────

HUMBLY SHEWETH,

   THAT, for several years, I applied myself to the study of Medicine, and obtained ─────────, conform to my Diploma, dated ─────────, that I herewith transmit Testimonials, and am willing to present myself for Examination before the Examiners of the College, and that, in the event of my being elected, I bind myself to observe the whole Laws and Regulations of the College,

> May it therefore please the Royal College, on the Council of the College and the Board of Examiners being satisfied, to admit me a Member of the College, with power to enjoy all the Rights, Liberties, and Privileges which any other Member does or may enjoy.

## No. IV.

A DIPLOMA in the following terms shall be granted to every FELLOW of the College.

"Collegium Regium Medicorum Edinburgense, rogante Præside, Sociisque annuentibus, decrevit ornatissimum virum A. B. in Societatem suam co-optare, et Collegam adsciscere. Ipsum ideo in societatem co-optat, Socium adsciscit, omniumque honorum atque privilegiorum quibus Socii ejusdem Collegii fruuntur, participem facit. In cujus rei fidem, hoc diploma, sigillo suo, Præsidis Secretariique chirographis munitum, expediri jussit.

"Actum Edinburgi, in Conventu Sociorum, die," etc.

## No. V.

A DIPLOMA in the following terms shall be granted to every MEMBER of the College.

"Collegium Regium Medicorum Edinburgense, rogante Præside Sociisque annuentibus, decrevit virum ornatissimum A. B. in ordinem Membrorum co-optare, et Membrum adsciscere. Ipsum ideo in ordinem Membrorum co-optat, Membrum adscisit, omniumque honorum atque privilegiorum, quibus Membra ejusdem Collegii fruuntur, participem facit.

"In cujus Rei fidem, hoc Diploma, sigillo suo, Præsidis Secretariique chirographis munitum, expediri jussit.

"Actum Edinburgi, in Conventu Sociorum, die," etc.

## No. VI.

A DIPLOMA, in the following terms, shall be granted to every LICENTIATE of the College.

"Collegium Regium Medicorum Edinburgense, rogante Præside, Sociisque annuentibus decrevit ornatum virum A. B. in numerum Permissorum co-optare. Ipsum ideo in numerum Permissorum co-optat, omniumque privilegiorum quibus Permissi ejusdem Collegii fruuntur, participem facit. In cujus rei fidem, hoc diploma, sigillo suo, Præsidis Secretariique chirographis munitum expediri jussit.

"Actum Edinburgi, in Conventu Sociorum," etc.

## No. VII.

FORM OF A CERTIFICATE to be presented by the College to Fellows who have been examined and found qualified to Lecture on any Branch of Medical Science required by the Examining Boards.

"Collegium Regium Medicorum Edinense, de―――― peracto examine, audita prælectione, inspectoque apparatu inter prælegendum adhibendo, his literis testatur docendo hanc Medicinæ partem virum ingenuum, consocium A. B. se parem comprobasse. In cujus rei fidem hanc chartam sigillo suo, Præsidis, Secretariique chirographo munitam, expediri jussit.

"Actum Edinburgi, in Conventu Sociorum, die," etc.

## Charta Erectionis
# REGII MEDICORUM COLLEGII
### APUD EDINBURGUM.

— — —

CAROLUS, Dei gratia, Magnæ Britanniæ Franciæ, et Hiberniæ Rex, Fideique Defensor, Omnibus probis hominibus suis ad quos præsentes Literæ pervenerint, salutem. SCIATIS, Quandoquidem nos, ex innata nostra bonitate, et erga populum nostrum paterna indulgentia, cum simus scilicet pater patriæ, et omnium legiorum et subditorum nostrorum parens nutritius, necnon maxime cupidi et provide curantes, ut non solum jura, proprietates, et possessiones, aliaque quævis subditorum nostrorum commoda rata, provisa, et confirmata sint, verum etiam (quæ maximi sunt pretii, et illorum maxime intersunt) ipsorum scilicet vita et sanitas, omnium aliorum externorum emolumentorum fundamentum et subjectum, Dei benedictione, media ordinaria, et honestorum, fidelium, et approbatorum medicorum diligentiam, et fideles conatus ad morbos tot et tam periculosos humanæ fragilitati contingentes curandos et præveniendos comitante, conservetur; necnon animo revolventes, quod legum aliarumque scientiarum praxis et artium, artificiorum et mechanicarum technarum exercitium, legibus cura et prudentia nostra, et Regiorum nostrorum prædecessorum tam commode regulata et disposita sit, ut nulli liceat aut permissum

*Preamble and reasons of foundation.*

*Importance of Life and Health*

*Importance of good Physicians*

*Examination of Candidates in other evers of other Profession.*

*Appendix.*

sit prius in lege tanquam jurisperitus, vel advocatus, vel in quovis alio munere aut officio eo spectante, vel in qualibet scientia, professione, aut arte practicare, quam per probatum examen capax et aptus inveniatur, perque viros sufficienti potestate et authoritate in hunc effectum instructos legitime admittatur: præ nimia tamen et ingenua nimis medicorum id temporis modestia (ne suo merito minus tribuere aut diffidere, aliorumve restrictionem in commodum et emolumentum suum intendere et designare videantur), physices et medicinæ praxis per longum tempus in maxima ataxia et confusione exstitit, et sine ullo warranto, authoritate, invasa, usurpata, proprioque impetu arrepta, exercita, magnaque in audacia et impunitate, sine ullo obstaculo aut impedimento, a mulierculis, alliisque non solum ignaris, sed et vilibus et sordidis personis, sine eruditione et liberali cultu, vel minima cujusvis literaturæ, ipsorumve medicinæ principiorum et elementorum notitia et tinctura, usa (potius abusa) fuit. Et non solum hortulani, aliique rudes et illiterati, in medicina practicare, et subditis nostris abuti, illudere, et imponere ausi sunt; verum etiam ad notitiam et famam prædictæ tolerationis et abusus peregrini impostores, agyrtæ, et empirici, nulla prævisa prohibitione, advenerunt, et in hoc regno diu commorati, et medicinam professi sunt et practicarunt, suaque medicamenta et pharmaca vendiderunt, et sine quovis vel ipsorum vel pharmacorum suorum conditionis et aptitudinis examine, populo distribuerunt. Quæquidem toleratio et abusus eo provecta est, ut quidam veneficii rei habiti et reputati professionem et praxin cum Doctoris Medicinæ nomine sibi assumere ausi sint; et quamvis ita plane rudes et ignari ut nec legere nec scribere queant, dictitare tamen audeant, et præscriptiones et receptas suas pro morborum maxime desperatorum cura

## Appendix. 147

describendas curent, cum magnis impensis, extortione, periculo, et destructione legiorum nostrorum, et in maximum dictæ professionis et scientiæ, tam antiquæ et necessariæ, tantique, per omnia tempora, et apud omnes nationes, usus et pretii, scandalum et opprobrium.

Cumque, ab exemplo et aliorum nostrorum regnorum, aliarumque bene constitutarum et gubernatarum nationum experientia, luculentur constet, quod Medicorum Societatis et Collegii ex personis gravibus, doctis, integris, et dictæ professioni congruentibus consistentis, erectio, maxime proprium et efficax foret medium, et ad tales abusus reformandos et præveniendos, ne in posterum irrepant, remedium ; cumque nos benignum habeamus affectum erga antiquam civitatem nostram Edinburgum, quæ non solum civium, sed et omnium subditorum nostrorum tantopere interest, cum, nempe, supremarum curiarum nostrarum juridicarum, in quibus authoritas et justitia nostra eminentissime repræsentantur et administrantur, sedes sit ordinaria, adeo ut nobilitas, ordoque equestris, aliique nostri subditi sæpe occasionem habeant, eoque ab omnibus regni angulis proficisci, inque dicta civitate, per tempora et tempestates morbis et intemperiebus maxime obnoxia , permanere teneantur, et considerationibus quibus supra Societatem et Collegium Medicorum modo, et cum potestatibus, facultatibus, et privilegiis infra script., Edinburgi erigere apud nos statuentes: Igitur nos dedimus et concessimus, tenoreque præsentium, ex certa nostra scientia, proprioque motu, prærogativa, et potestate nostra regali, damus et concedimus Davidi Hay, Thomæ Burnet, Matheo Brisbaine, Archibaldo Stevensone, Andreæ Balfoure, Roberto Sibbald, Jacobo Livingstone, Roberto Crawfurd, Roberto Trotter, Matheo Sinclare, Jacobo Stewart, Gulielmo Stevensone,

*And all this to the manifest injury of the Public.*

*The erection of a College of Physicians is the most appropriate means of reforming such abuses*

*Peculiarly necessary in Edinburgh is the Metropolis and seat of the Courts of Law.*

*College of Physicians to be erected.*

*First Fellows named in Charter.*

Alexandro Cranstone, Joanni Hutton, Joanni M'Gill, Gulielmo Lauder, Joanni Lermonth, Jacobo Halket, Gulielmo Wright, Patricio Halyburton, et Archibaldo Pitcairne, artium magistris, et medicinæ doctoribus, omnibusque aliis qui posthac ab illis in ipsorum societatem cooptati fuerint, et ab illis tanquam collegæ et sodales eorum societatis intra dictam nostram urbem Edinburgi, suburbia et privilegia ejusdem, admissi fuerint, ut in unum corpus, communitatem, et Collegium uniantur et conjungantur omni tempore futuro.

Et creximus, instituimus, et incorporavimus, tenoreque præsentium erigimus, instituimus, et incorporamus viros supra mentionatos, eorumque successores, Collegium, societatem, et incorporationem fieri omni tempore futuro, omnibusque potestatibus, facultatibus, et privilegiis ad liberum Collegium, societatem, et incorporationem requisitis et spectantibus, frui et habere, et absque præjudicio generalitatis prædictæ, quocunque loco et tempore, et quoties sibi visum fuerit, convenire; cumque potestate illis, eorumque successoribus, commune gazophylacium seu thesaurarium et patrimonium habendi, et voluntaria munera, contributiones, legata, et donationes, in commodum et usum dicti Collegii, et ad medicinæ professionem et physices praxin et exercitium proferendum et promovendum impendendi, inter se erogandi, et ab aliis benevolis accipiendi. Inque hunc effectum, iisdem potestatem tradimus, eosque capaces reddimus, acquirendi, procurandi, habendi, et terras, tenementa, annuos-reditus, possessiones, decimas, aliaque in usum dicti Collegii, ejusque collegarum successorum, cum intra tum extra burgum, possidendi, et commune sigillum habendi, commune Sigillum Regii Medicorum Collegii apud Edinburgum designandum, et habendi, agendi, et exercendi omnes alias libertates, potestates, et facultates cuilibet alii libero collegio et incorporationi competentes, quasve ipsi tanquam corpora incorporata debent, seu habere, agere, aut exercere poterint. All the ordinary privileges of Corporate Bodies

Et pro meliori dicti collegii regimine, et thesauri et patrimonii eidem spectaturi administratione, dedimus, tenoreque præsentium dictæ societati et Collegio potestatem damus, ejusdemque collegis mandamus, annuatim, omni tempore futuro, Concilium, ex septem dictæ societatis collegarum doctissimis, sapientissimis, et in facultate medicinæ maxime peritis, consistens, eligere: Quod quidem concilium unum ex eorum numero, pro illo anno Præsidem fore est electurum; cum potestate etiam dicto Præsidi et Concilio, Clericum, Thesaurarium aliosque Ministros in commodum dictæ societatis necessaiios et requisitos, eligendi et constituendi. Et declaramus dictum Præsidem, Collegium, et communitatem, sub nomine *Præsidis Regii Medicorum Collegii apud Edinburgum* capacem fore causas coram omnibus et quibuscunque judicibus in quibuscunque curiis et actionibus agere, prosequi, et tueri. Ac ulterius dicto Præsidi et Collegio, eorumque successoribus, potestatem tradimus, canones, præcepta, acta, et statuta sanciendi ad medicinæ scientiam promovendam, ejusdem praxin rite disponendam, inque bonam gubernationem, ordinem, regimen, et correctionem dicti Collegii et communitatis, omniumque dictam facultatem exercentium intra dictam civitatem Edinburgenam, ejusque suburbia, solummodo, viz., Letham, Vicum Canonicorum, Portam Occidentalem, Vicum Sancti Leonardi, et Vicum Figulinum, quando, et quotiescunque necesse fuerit. Proviso omnino, sicuti per præsentes providetur et declaratur, quod præsentibus non obstantibus Pharmaco-chirurgi Edinburgenses potestatem habituri sunt, omne genus vulnerum, con-

*Side notes:* Government of College. Council of Seven. President. Secretary, Treasurer, and other Officers. College may be a party in actions at law. College may make Bye Laws for promoting the Sciences and regulating Practice of Medicine. Also for its own regulation and that of all Practitioners within its jurisdiction.

tusionum, fracturarum, dislocationum, tumorum, ulcerum, et id genus alia quæ sunt chirurgicarum operationum subjecta, et accidentia exinde orientia duntaxat curandi; curam autem morborum originaliter internorum, ex medicorum dicti Collegii præscripto et directione unice præstandam, minime habebunt.

Et similiter concessimus, tenoreque præsentium concedimus, præfato Præsidi et Collegio, eorumque successoribus quod nulli intra dictam civitatem, ejusque suburbia et privilegia, antedictam facultatem prius practicare et exercere licebit, quam ad eandem per dictum Præsidem et Collegium, eorumque pro tempore successores, warranto et diplomate in hunc effectum per dictum Præsidem et Collegium, eorumque pro tempore successores concesso, eorumque communi sigillo signato fuerit admissus; idque sub pœna sexaginta librarum monetæ Scotiæ, quovis mense quo quicunque, modo prædicto nondum licentiatus, et admissus, dicta facultate et praxi utetur et exercebit. Quarum quidem mulctarum alterum dimidium pauperum, alterum dicti Collegii usui et commodo applicandum volumus. Si quivis tamen, post censuram modo prædicto, dictam facultatem nihilominus absque licentia exercere persistet prædictam mulctam, quovis mense, quo practicare persistent, duplicandam ordinamus.

Et pariter volumus, concedimus, et ordinamus, quod annuatim duo ex dicta Societate et Collegio per dictum concilium tanquam Censores eligantur, qui cum Præside pro tempore, vice et nomine dicti Collegii, potestatem, authoritatem, et jurisdictionem habebunt, omnes dictam medicinæ facultatem absque licentia, ut prædicitur, intra prædictam civitatem, libertates, et suburbia prædicta practicantes et exercentes, coram sese convocandi, illisque mulctas supra specificatas imponendi; dicto tamen medicorum Collegio, ejusve Præside, curias ad delinquentes puniendos tenturo, præpositum civitatis Edinburgi, vel unum aliquem ex ejusdem magistratibus, de curiæ suæ loco et tempore omni modo certiorem faciente, adeo ut (si ipsis visum fuerit) unum ex balivis suis illis in jurisdictione cumulativa assidere constituent: Proviso omnimodo, sicuti per præsentes providetur et declaratur, quod medicorum Collegio nondum licebit quemvis pharmaco-chirurgum Edinburgi burgensem mulctare, sine consensu præpositi, aut cujusvis unius ex balivis Edinburgi, qui assidebit, et talibus actis judicialibus intererit. Et si venire et adesse abnuerint, hoc secreto nostro concilio notum faciendum est, ut hi quod idoneum et justum sit, perficiant, absque præjudicio dicto Collegio, in casu recusationis et moræ procedendi, et similiter invigilandi, gubernandi, et coram se convocandi, et, si necesse fuerit, corrigendi et puniendi omnes medicos, et medicinæ doctores associatos, seu licentiatos, dictam facultatem intra dictam civitatem, et limites prædictos, exercentes, ob quæcunque crimina et delicta ab illis in eorum praxi contra statuta et acta dicti Collegii commissa; idque ab illis talia amerciamenta et mulctas exigendo, ut dicto Præsidi, Censoribus, et supervisoribus visum fuerit, utque delictum promerebitur; dictis tamen mulctis summam quadraginta librarum nondum excedentibus: quæ quidem amerciamenta et mulctæ usibus prædictis applicanda volumus et ordinamus. Et pro iisdem namando, et omni alia executione legali utendo et incarcerando, et ad sententias et mandata de tempore in tempus per dictos supervisores, virtute potestatis et authoritatis illis per nos commissæ, emittenda, magistratus intra dictam civitatem, suburbia et libertates ejusdem prædictas, aliosque nostros legis ministros, per præsentes, authoritate nostra mandamus et requirimus, ad prædictas sententias exequendas assistere ; inque hunc effectum, præcepta namationis, aliasque executiones necessarias dirigere, eodem modo quo super propriis suis decretis et sententiis agere solent ; cum potestate etiam dictis Præsidi et Censoribus, quoties opus fuerit, scrutandi, considerandi, et inspiciendi pharmaca, et medicamenta simplicia et composita nunc aut in posterum vendenda intra dictam civitatem, suburbia, et libertates prædictas, si recentia, bona, et proba sint, et quæ secure ad morbos et infirmitates legiorum nostrorum curandos usurpari et applicari poterint. Proviso omnimodo, sicuti per præsentes specialiter providetur, quod ubi talis inspectio et scrutinium faciendum est, unus ex magistratibus intra dictam civitatem, cum uno pharmacopœo et chirurgo-pharmacopœo, visitoribus pro tempore constituendis, qui assistere requirantur, ut eadem bene, et secundum regulas, pro populi commodo composita et præparata esse videant ; et ubi pharmaca insufficientia et corrupta invenientur, cum potestate illis eadem in publicas plateas ejiciendi, vel destruendi.

Et ulterius, pro nobis et successoribus nostris volumus et concedimus, quod neque Præses, neque quivis alius dicti Medicorum Collegii, neve eorum successores, super assisam aut inquisitionem in urbe aut rure procedere citentur aut summoniantur. Cumque eorum in ægrotos et valetudinarios observantia sit semper adeo necessaria, ut sine maximo præjudicio et ægrotorum periculo ab eadem quovis pretextu et occasione abstrahi non debeant ; igitur nos, pro nobis et successoribus nostris, dictum Præsidem, omnesque dicti Collegii socios et collegas eorumque successores, ab omnibus excubiis in futurum liberamus et absolvimus.

Et per præsentes declaramus, quodvis jus, protestatem, et jurisdictionem ad magistratus civitatis Edinburgi, et quævis jura et privilegia ad chirurgo-pharma-

## Appendix.

copœos pertinentia, illis et singulis eorum respective, prout de jure competit, specialiter reservari.

Per præsentes etiam specialiter providetur, jurium et privilegiorum supra scriptorum dicto Medicorum Collegio concessionem, ad scholarum pro dicta arte medica, aut qualibet ejusdem parte docenda erectionem, seu gradus alicui eatenus conferendos et concedendos, nullo modo extendendam; eadem per præsentes specialiter declaratur absque præjudicio fore jurium et privilegiorum in favorem Universitatis seu Collegii Andreapolitani, Glasguensis, Abredonensis, et Edinburgensis concessorum; et præsentibus, et clausulis quibuscunque inibi contentis non obstantibus, licitum et legitimum erit cuivis in dictis universitatibus laurea doctorandis, libertatem et potestatem habere in dicta civitate aliisque locis supra scriptis practicandi, ipsis tamen prædictis mulctis aliisque pœnis supra scriptis nondum obnoxiis, nisi intra dictos limites, vel quamlibet earundem partem, actu commorati fuerint; in quo casu, dictæ incorporationis et societatis præceptis et regulis, sicut alii in eadem incorporati, solummodo subjicientur: et dictum Medicorum Collegium, more prædicto erigendum, per præsentes obligatur quemvis hominem seu homines in dictis Universitatibus laurea doctorandos, absque quovis prævio seu antecedente examine, sed solummodo ad ipsorum diplomatis, seu ad gradus admissionis Præsidi dicti Medicorum Collegii productionem licentiare.

Per præsentes omnimodo specialiter providetur, quod jurium et privilegiorum supra scriptorum dicto Medicorum Collegio concessio nullo modo præjudicabit quemvis artium magistri gradum in qualibet dicti regni universitate nactum, et statim medicinæ praxin exercentem, vel ad doctoris gradum in quavis ex prædictis universitatibus, seu qualibet celebri universitate extera admissum, quo minus viri hisce qualitatibus instructi, ad literarum suarum patentium a dictis universitatibus domi aut peregre Præsidi dicti Collegii productionem, intra limites præscriptos practicare licentientur, nullo præeunte examine.

*Professors of Medicine in the Universities shall be admitted as Fellows.*

Specialiter itidem providetur, quod publici medicinæ professores respectivarum universitatum hujus regni, ad eorum Præsidi Collegii supplicationem, tanquam socii honorarii ejusdem societatis admittentur.

Et postremo, fideliter promittimus in verbo Principis, hoc præsens diploma in hoc currenti Parliamento ratificatum iri, et per præsentes status Parliamenti idem conformiter ratificari requirimus. In cujus rei testimonium, præsentibus magnum Sigillum nostrum appendi mandavimus, apud aulam nostram de Whitehall, vigesimo nono die mensis Novembris, anno Domini millesimo sexcentesimo octogesimo primo, et anno regni nostri trigesimo tertio.

*Promise of Ratification.*

Per signaturam manu S. D. N. Regis suprascriptam.

# Charter of Ratification

IN FAVOUR OF THE

# ROYAL COLLEGE OF PHYSICIANS,

EDINBURGH.

*Dated June 16, 1685.*

---

*At Edinburgh, the Sixteenth day of June, One Thousand Six Hundred eighty and five years.*

OUR SOVEREIGN LORD, with advice and consent of the Estates of this present Parliament, ratifies and approves, and for his Majesty and his successors perpetually confirms, the Letters-patent granted by his Majesty's dearest brother, King CHARLES the Second, of ever blessed memory, whereof the tenor follows.

*Ratification and approval of Charter.*

[*Here the Letters-Patent are engrossed* verbatim.]

Together with all acts, decreets, and sentences of his Majesty's Privy Council, or of the Lords of Session, or of any other judicatory within this kingdom, conceived in favour of the Royal College of Physicians, for making the Patent above written, and privileges therein contained, effectual: And specially, but prejudice of the generality, an act of his Majesty's Privy Council, of the date the twenty-first day of November, one thousand six hundred eighty and four years, ordaining the said Royal College, at least twice a-year, to visit all

*Ratification of Act of Privy Council, 1684, ordaining the C[ollege] to visit [etc.]*

apothecaries' shops and chambers within Edinburgh, suburbs and liberties thereof, calling to their assistance one or two of the eldest or ablest of the brotherhood of the apothecaries; as also, that they desire one of the Bailies of Edinburgh, or respective Magistrates of the place where the shops to be visited do lie, to grant their concurrence in the said visitation; and these Bailies or Magistrates are, by the said act, ordained, upon any such desire, to grant their effectual concurrence for ejecting and destroying all corrupt and insufficient drugs; and also ordaining, that the apothecaries, when required, shall attend and assist the said physicians; and that all masters of apothecaries' shops or chambers, or their servants, receive these visitors of the shops with all respect, and expose to their view all the drugs that shall be called for; and that upon oath, to be administered both to themselves and servants; and shall quietly and peaceably suffer the drugs that shall be found insufficient by the said physicians to be ejected and destroyed, as they will be answerable; And sicklike, ordaining that no persons who have not already been examined and admitted by the fraternity of apothecaries, be suffered in any time coming, by the Magistrates aforesaid, to keep any apothecaries' shops or chambers, except such allenarly as shall be tried and approven by the President and Censors of the said Royal College: And in like manner, ane act of the Lords of Session, dated the twenty-first day of March last bypast, proceeding upon suspension, at the instance of an chirurgeon-apothecary, of a sentence pronounced by the President and Censors of the said Royal College, for unwarrantable practice of Medicine: whereby it was found by the said Lords of Session, that where the Magistrates of Edinburgh refuse or delay or give concurrence to punish delinquents, that the College, in that case, have both the judicative and executive power, in all and sundry heads, points, articles, circumstances, and conditions, contained in the said Letters-patent, and act above mentioned, and after the terms and tenor thereof, in all points: And his Majesty, with advice and consent foresaid, wills and grants, and for his Majesty and his successors, decerns and ordains, That this present ratification is, and shall be, as valid, sufficient and effectual, to the said Royal College, and their successors, as if the acts above mentioned were herein at length *de verbo in verbum* specially insert and engrossed: Whereanent our said Sovereign Lord, with advice and consent foresaid, for his Majesty and his successors, hath dispensed, and by their presents dispenses for ever.—Extracted forth of the Records of Parliament, by George Viscount of Tarbat, Lord M'Leod and Castlehaven, Clerk to his Majesty's Parliament, Council Registers and Rolls, &c.

TARBAT, CLER. REG.

ROYAL WARRANT

FOR

# Charter of Incorporation

IN FAVOUR OF THE

# ROYAL COLLEGE OF PHYSICIANS
## OF EDINBURGH,

*16th August* 1861.

---

### VICTORIA R.

VICTORIA, by the Grace of God, of the United Kingdom of Great Britain and Ireland, Queen; Defender of the Faith:

Whereas the Royal College of Physicians of Edinburgh have, by their Petition, humbly represented unto Us that our Royal Predecessor Charles the Second was pleased to erect and incorporate the said College by Charter or Letters Patent, bearing date at Whitehall, the twenty-ninth day of November, one thousand six hundred and eighty-one, in the thirty-third year of his reign, which Charter was afterwards ratified, approved, and confirmed by an Act of the Scottish Parliament, bearing date the sixteenth day of June, one thousand six hundred and eighty-five; and that the establishment of the said College has fulfilled the high purposes of consolidating the medical profession, elevating its character and dignity, and encouraging and advancing medical learning and science: And whereas the said College have also represented unto Us, that by an Act passed in the twenty-first and twenty-second year of our reign, intituled, "An Act to regulate the Qualifications of Practitioners in Medicine and Surgery," it was enacted that it should be lawful for Us to grant to the Corporation of the Royal College of Physicians of Edinburgh a new Charter, and thereby to give to the said College of Physicians the name of "The Royal College of Physicians of Scotland," and that it should be lawful for the said Royal College of Physicians, under their Common Seal, to accept such new Charter, and that such acceptance should operate as a surrender of all Charters heretofore granted to the said corporation; and that by another Act, passed in the twenty-second year of our reign, intituled "An Act to amend the Medical Act (1858)," it was enacted that the term "Member" should be added to the Qualifications described in the schedule to the first-mentioned Act, in reference to the said College; and further, that by another Act, passed in the twenty-third and twenty-fourth year of our reign, intituled, "An Act to amend the Medical Act (1858)," it was enacted that any new Charter to be granted to the said College, may be granted either by and in its present name, or, as provided by the Medical Act, by and in the name of the Royal College of Physicians of Scotland: And whereas the said College have further represented to Us that the said Charter granted by our Royal Predecessor contains various provisions, which, by reason of the great changes that have taken place in the practice of medicine, have altogether gone into desuetude, and that it is expedient, and would be for the benefit of the said College, and of the medical profession, that a new Charter should be granted to the said College, by and in its present name, in pursuance of the provisions of the said Acts: Now know ye, that We, taking the premises into our Royal consideration of our especial grace, certain knowledge, and mere motion, have given, granted, and ordained, and by these presents, for Us, our heirs and successors, do give, grant, and ordain, as follows (that is to say):—

*New Charter to be given to the College in its present name.*

I. Alexander Wood, Doctor of Medicine, President; James Young Simpson, Doctor of Medicine, Vice-President; and Peter Fairbairn, William Seller, Charles Bell, William Henry Lowe, Alexander Keiller, and William Tennant Gairdner, Members of the Council of the said College, and their successors in office, and the other existing Fellows of the said College, and all other persons who shall hereafter be admitted or elected Fellows and Members of the said College, as hereinafter provided, shall be and are hereby united and incorporated into one body politic and corporate, by the name of "The Royal College of Physicians of Edinburgh," and shall by that name have perpetual succession, and a Common Seal, with power to break, alter, and renew the same from time to time, and may by that name sue and be sued; and the College shall at all times hereafter be capable in law to take, purchase, possess, hold, and enjoy, for the uses and purposes of the College, any lands, tenements, or other heritages, and personal estate not exceeding in the whole the yearly value of Ten Thousand Pounds, and, if necessary to sell, dispone, and convey the same, and to lend money on heritable or moveable, real or personal securities, and to hold goods and chattels for the uses and purposes of the

*First Fellows named in Charter.*

*Power of College to have Common Seal;*

*to hold Lands, etc.*

College; and all charters, dispositions, securities, and other deeds or instruments affecting heritable or moveable, real or personal property, to be granted in favour of the College, may be taken in their corporate name, or to Trustees, on behalf of the College; and all charters, dispositions, or other deeds or instruments to be granted by the College, shall be under the Common Seal, and shall be subscribed by three of the Trustees, and by the President, or Treasurer, or Secretary of the College, for the time being.

II. All property, heritable and moveable, real and personal, wheresoever situated, and all feu-charters, dispositions, bonds, instruments of sasine, leases, agreements, and other deeds and instruments, and vouchers of such property, or relating thereto, which have been already acquired by, or taken, granted, or executed in favour of the said Royal College of Physicians of Edinburgh, or any person or persons, as Trustee or Trustees, or otherwise, for the use or on behalf of the said College, whether the same be held absolutely or in security, and in general all estate and effects, and all debts, obligations, rights, interests, liberties, privileges, and immunities of and belonging to the said College, or vested in any person or persons for the benefit of the said College at the time of the granting of these presents, shall be, and the same are hereby transferred to and vested in the Royal College of Physicians of Edinburgh hereby Incorporated, as fully as if the same had been acquired by, or taken, granted, or executed in favour of the College after the granting of these presents; and the same shall in future be held, managed, sold, conveyed, assigned, leased, discharged, or otherwise disposed of by the College, under their corporate name of "The Royal College of Physicians of Edinburgh," without the necessity of any connecting or continuing title, or separate investiture, or writing, or procedure, other than these presents.

III. The existing Fellows of the Royal College of Physicians of Edinburgh, at the time of the granting of these presents, shall be the first Fellows of the College hereby incorporated.

*Existing Fellows to be first Fellows of the College.*

IV. The Fellows may, from time to time, elect and admit to be Fellows and Members of the College such persons as they shall think fit and qualified, in such manner, at such times, under such regulations, and on payment of such fees, as may, from time to time, be directed by the bye-laws.

*Fellows to have power to elect Fellows and Members.*

V. The Fellows may, from time to time, admit to be Licentiates of the College, any persons who shall have gone through such course of studies, and passed such examinations, or submitted to such other regulations, and paid such fees, as may, from time to time, be directed by the bye-laws; and the existing Licentiates of the Royal College of Physicians of Edinburgh, at the time of the granting of these presents, shall be Licentiates of the College hereby incorporated.

*Fellows to have power to admit Licentiates.*

VI. If it shall at any time hereafter appear that any Fellow, Member, or Licentiate of the College has obtained admission to or license from the College, or the Royal College of Physicians of Edinburgh, by any fraud, false statement, or imposition, or that he has violated any bye-law, rule, or regulation of the College, then, and in every such case, and after such previous notice to, and such hearing of, such Fellow, Member, or Licentiate, as under the circumstances the Council shall think proper, it shall be lawful for the Fellows, with the concurrence of not less than three-fourths of their number, present at a Meeting, specially summoned for the purpose, to pass such censure or sentence of suspension against the Fellow,

*Fellows to have power of suspension or expulsion of Fellows, Members, or Licentiates.*

*Procedure for suspension or expulsion.*

Member, or Licentiate so offending, as shall be determined at such meeting, or to expel such Fellow, Member, or Licentiate from the College; and upon any such sentence of suspension or expulsion being passed, such Fellow, Member, or Licentiate shall cease to be a Fellow, Member, or Licentiate of the College, and to have any right or interest in or to the property or funds of the College, either absolutely, or for such time as shall be specified in the sentence of suspension; and all the rights and privileges granted to such Fellow, Member, or Licentiate, as the case may be, shall cease and determine upon such expulsion or during such suspension.

*Ordinary Meetings of Fellows.*

VII. Ordinary Meetings of the Fellows, for the transaction of the business of the College, shall be held at such times as shall, from time to time, be fixed by the bye-laws.

*Extraordinary Meetings of Fellows.*

VIII. Extraordinary Meetings of the Fellows, for the consideration and disposal of any special business of the College, may be called by the President or the Council at any time when the same shall be deemed necessary; and it shall be incumbent on the President to call an Extraordinary Meeting of the Fellows on a requisition to that effect, specifying the purpose of such Meeting, and signed by any five of the Fellows, being delivered to him or to the Secretary of the College; and notice of all Extraordinary Meetings of the Fellows shall be given in such manner as shall be directed by the Bye-Laws.

*Ordinary Meetings of Fellows and Members.*

IX. Ordinary Meetings of the Fellows and Members for the consideration of matters affecting the general interests of the medical profession and the public, shall be held at such times as shall from time to time be fixed by the Bye-Laws.

*Extraordinary Meetings of Fellows and Members.*

X. Extraordinary Meetings of the Fellows and Members may be called by the President or the Council at any time when the same shall be deemed necessary; and it shall be incumbent on the President to call an Extraordinary Meeting of the Fellows and Members on a requisition to that effect, specifying the purpose of such Meeting, and signed by any five of the Fellows or Members, being delivered to him or to the Secretary of the College; and notice of all Extraordinary Meetings of the Fellows and Members shall be given in such manner as shall be directed by the Bye-Laws; and any matters affecting the general interests of the medical profession and the public, which shall be specified in such requisition and notice, may be considered at any such Extraordinary Meeting of Fellows and Members.

XI. The Council of the College shall consist of the President and six of the Fellows resident in Edinburgh, or within seven miles of the General Post-Office in Edinburgh, by the nearest public highway. *(Council of College)*

XII. A meeting of the Fellows shall be held annually, on such day and at such hour as may, from time to time, be fixed by the Bye-Laws, for the election of the President and the Members of the Council. *(Meeting for election of President and Council.)*

XIII. The Council shall elect the Examiners of the College, and shall also elect a Treasurer, Secretary, Clerk, and such other officers as may be deemed necessary, annually, and as often as occasion may require, or vacancies occur, by death, resignation, or otherwise. *(Council to elect Office-Bearers.)*

XIV. The Council shall, with the approval of the Fellows, nominate four Fellows, who, along with the Treasurer, shall be Trustees for the College; and as often as a vacancy shall arise by death, resignation, or otherwise, the Council shall fill up the same; and the existing Trustees of the said College at the time of the granting of these presents, shall be the first Trustees under these presents. *(Trustees.)*

*Appendix.*

*Existing Officers to continue in Office till first Meeting.*

XV. The existing Members of the Council of the said College at the time of the granting of these presents shall continue in office, and be the first Council of the College under these presents; and the existing President shall continue in office, and be the first President of the College under these presents; and the existing Treasurer, Secretary, Clerk, and other officers of the said College shall continue to hold their several offices until the first Annual Meeting of the Fellows for the election of the Members of the Council and the President, to be held after the granting of these presents.

*Vacancies in the Presidentship or Council may be filled up by Fellows.*

XVI. If it shall happen that any election of the President or of the Members of the Council, or any of them, shall not be made on the day appointed for that purpose, or if any Fellow elected to any such office shall not accept thereof, the person or persons then filling such office or offices shall continue to fill the same until another person or persons shall be appointed thereto; and the Fellows present at any Ordinary Meeting, or at an Extraordinary Meeting, to be called as herein provided, may elect out of the Fellows a person or persons to fill the said office or offices, or such of them as shall not have been filled up, or shall be vacant by reason of non-acceptance as aforesaid, for such part of the year of office as shall be then unexpired.

*Filling of vacancies caused by Death or Resignation.*

XVII. If the President or any Member of the Council shall die or resign before the expiration of the year, or other time for which he shall have been elected, the Fellows present at any Ordinary Meeting, or at an Extraordinary Meeting to be called as herein provided, may elect out of the Fellows a President or Member of the Council, as the case may be, in the place or stead of the President or Member of the Council so dying or resigning; and the Fellow or Fellows so elected shall serve for the remainder of the year of office, or other time, for which the President or Member of the Council so dying or resigning was elected.

XVIII. The property and affairs of the College shall be managed and administered by the Fellows and the Council, in such manner, and under such regulations, as may from time to time be directed by the Bye-Laws.

*Management of property and affairs of College.*

XIX. All acts done by the President, or by any Meeting of the Council, or by any person acting as President or Member of the Council, shall, notwithstanding it may be afterwards discovered that there was any defect or informality in the election or appointment of any such President or Member of the Council acting as aforesaid, or that they, or any of them, were or was disqualified, or that there was any vacancy in the office of President, or in the Council, be as valid as if every such person had been duly elected or appointed and was duly qualified, and as if no such vacancy had existed.

*Acts of President not to be invalidated by any informality in their election.*

XX. It shall be lawful for the Fellows, and We do hereby grant full power and authority to them, from time to time, to make Bye-Laws, Rules, and Regulations, for promoting the Science of Medicine, for duly ordering the practice of the same, and for the good government, order and direction of the College; for the admission and election of Fellows, Members, and Licentiates, and fixing and defining the qualifications of persons to be so admitted and elected; for the management of the property, funds, and affairs of the College; for the regulation of all meetings, actings, and proceedings of the College, and of the Council and Fellows, and of the Fellows and Members, and of the several Office-Bearers

*Fellows to have power to make Bye-Laws.*

and Officers of the College, and fixing the times for holding such meetings; and for the division of the persons composing the body corporate of the College into such orders of Resident and Non-resident Fellows or Members, or otherwise; and for giving and assigning to these orders such qualifications, powers, privileges, exemptions, and restrictions, as the Fellows may from time to time determine; and it shall be lawful for the Fellows, from time to time, to repeal, vary, or alter such Bye-Laws, Rule, and Regulations: Provided that every Bye-Law, Rules, and Regulation to be hereafter made, and every repeal, variation, or alteration of any existing Bye-Law, Rule, or Regulation, shall be submitted to and approved by an Ordinary or Extraordinary Meeting of the Fellows, in such form and manner as they shall from time to time direct and appoint.

<small>All new Rules or any change to be approved by a Meeting of the Fellows.</small>

XXI. The Bye-Laws, Rules, and Regulations of the said Royal College of Physicians of Edinburgh existing and in force at the time of the granting of these presents, except in so far as the same may be inconsistent with these presents, shall be and continue to be the Bye-Laws, Rules, and Regulations of the College hereby incorporated, until the same are repealed, altered, or varied, in whole or in part.

<small>Existing Bye-Laws to continue in force unless inconsistent with this Charter.</small>

XXII. The College hereby incorporated, and the Fellows, Members, and Licentiates thereof, shall and may have, exercise, and enjoy all such powers, functions, rights, and privileges, as the said Royal College of Physicians of Edinburgh, or the Fellows, Members, or Licentiates thereof respectively, before the granting of these presents, had or might have had, exercised or enjoyed under and by virtue of the several Acts of our reign hereinbefore recited.

<small>College to have same powers as it possessed before the granting of this Charter.</small>

XXIII. The following words and expressions in these presents shall have the several meanings hereby assigned to them; that is to say:—

The expression "the College" shall mean "The Royal College of Physicians of Edinburgh," hereby incorporated; the words "Council," "Fellows," "Members," and "Licentiates," shall respectively mean the Council, Fellows, Members, and Licentiates of the College for the time being; and the word "Bye-Laws" shall mean and include the Bye-Laws, Rules, and Regulations of the College, made *or to be made, as herein* provided. Interpretation Clause.

And with the consent of the College, testified by their acceptance of these presents, and by the authority of the Act of Our reign first before recited, We do hereby accept the surrender made to Us by the Royal College of Physicians of Edinburgh of the said Charter or Letters Patent granted by our Royal Predecessor King Charles the Second, and do hereby revoke, annul, and make void the same: And We do hereby, for Us, our heirs and successors, further grant to the College, that this our Charter shall be in and by all things valid and effectual in law, according to the true intent and meaning of the same, and shall be held, construed, and adjudged in the most favourable and beneficial sense, and for the best advantage of the College, notwithstanding any misrecital, defect, uncertainty, or imperfections whatsoever: And We do hereby, for Us, our heirs and successors, covenant, grant, and agree to and with the College, that We, our heirs and successors, shall and will, from time to time, and at all times hereafter, upon their humble suit and request, give and grant to the College all such further and other powers, privileges, and authorities for Old Charter revoked.

rendering more effectual this our grant, according to the true intent and meaning of these presents, as We, our heirs and successors, can or may lawfully grant, and as shall be reasonably advised and devised by the Council learned in the law of the College for the time being.

And We further will and command that this our Charter do pass the Seal appointed by the Treaty of Union to be kept and used in Scotland in place of the Great Seal thereof per saltum, without passing any other Seal or Register: For which these presents shall be, as well to the Director of our Chancery for writing the same, as to the Keeper of the said Seal for causing the said Seal to be appended thereto, a sufficient warrant.

Given, at our Court at Saint James's the sixteenth day of August 1861, in the Twenty-fifth year of our reign.

By Her Majesty's Command,

G. GREY.

# Charta Incorporationis

IN FAVOREM

# COLLEGII REGII MEDICORUM

## EDINENSIS.

### 1861.

---

VICTORIA, Dei gratia Britanniarum Regina; Fidei Defensor; OMNIBUS probis hominibus ad quos præsentes literæ Nostræ pervenerint salutem:

QUUM Nobis Collegium Regium Medicorum Edinense, petitione sua, reverentissime ostendisset, placuisse Regio Nostro Antecessori Carolo Secundo, Charta sive Literis Patentibus, in Aula apud Whitehall datis, vigesimo nono die mensis Novembris anno Domini millesimo sexcentesimo octogesimo primo, anno regni illius trigesimo tertio, dictum Collegium constituere et incorporare : et eandem chartam postea, per Actum Parliamenti Scotiæ latum, die decimo sexto mensis Junii, anno Domini millesimo sexcentesimo octogesimo quinto, sancitam, approbatam, et confirmatam fuisse : necnon ejusdem Collegii institutionem, medicinæ professionem consolidando, gratiam dignitatemque ejus attollendo,

*Preamble and History of Foundation.*

*Success of College in advancing Medical Science.*

doctrinam scientiamque medicam suscitando atque promovendo, gravia implevisse consilia. ET QUUM Nobis dictum Collegium quoque ostendisset, decretum esse per actum latum, vigesimo primo et vigesimo secundo annis Nostri regni, cui titulus est, vernaculo sermone, "An Act to regulate the Qualifications of Practitioners in Medicine and Surgery," ut Nobis liceat novam concedere Chartam Collegio Regio Medicorum Edinensi, in qua charta, dicto Collegio nomen, vernaculo sermone, "The Royal College of Physicians of Scotland," daretur, utque dicto Collegio liceat novam hanc Chartam sub sigillo suo communi accipere, qua quidem accepta, id ipsum pro deditione omnium Chartarum catenus dicto Collegio concessarum haberetur : porro decretum esse per aliud actum latum, anno Nostri regni vigesimo secundo, cui, vernaculo

*Medical Act of 1858.*

sermone, titulus est, "An Act to amend the Medical Act (1858)," ut verbum, vernaculo sermone, "Member," qualificationibus enumeratis in schedula acti primum recitati quatenus ad dictum Collegium attinet, adjiceretur : deinde autem decretum esse per aliud actum latum, vigesimo tertio et vigesimo quarto annis Nostri regni, cui titulus est, vernaculo sermone, "An Act to amend the Medical Act (1858)," ut quaecunque nova Charta dicto Collegio concederetur, concedi possit, vel ex et sub praesenti ejus nomine, vel, sicuti provisum est in Acto cui, vernaculo sermone, titulus est, "The Medical Act," ex et sub nomine, "The Royal College of Physicians of Scotland."

*Changes required in Original Charter.*

ET QUUM praeterea Nobis dictum Collegium ostendisset dictam Chartam a Regio Nostro Antecessore concessam quaedam in se habere provisa, quae, propter ingentes in medicinae arte mutationes, prorsus obsoleverint ; necnon et convenire et beneficio fore dicto Collegio et medicinae professioni, novam dicto Collegio

Chartam concedere, ex et sub præsenti ejus nomine, quatenus licet per recitatorum Actorum decreta. NUNC SCIATIS: Nos hæc præmissa animo Nostro Nobiscum versantes, singulari ex gratia, vera opinione, meroque motu, DEDIMUS CONCESSIMUS et ORDINAVIMUS et his præsentibus literis pro Nobis, pro Nostris heredibus, et pro Nostris successoribus, DAMUS CONCEDIMUS et ORDINAMUS, quæ sequuntur, scilicet: *[New Charter to be given to the College in its present name.]*

1. Alexandrum Wood, Medicinæ Doctorem, Præsidem; Jacobum Young Simpson, Medicinæ Doctorem, Vicepræsidis; et Petrum Fairbairn, Gulielmum Seller, Carolum Bell, Gulielmum Henricum Lowe, Alexandrum Keiller, et Gulielmum Tennant Gairdner, qui Concilii dicti Collegii sunt, et illorum successores in eo munere; necnon ceteros dicti Collegii exsistentes Socios, aliosque omnes, quicunque posthac dicti Collegii Socii, et Membra admissi aut electi fuerint, ut postea provisum sit, conjunctum iri et in unum corpus politicum et incorporatum constitutum iri, et hac charta revera conjungi et in unum corpus politicum et incorporatum constitui sub nomine, "The Royal College of Physicians of Edinburgh;" eosque, eo nomine, perpetuam habituros successionem, et sigillum commune cum potestate idem frangendi mutandi et renovandi identidem, et eosdem, sub eo nomine, in jus vocare et in jus vocari posse. Et, omni futuro tempore, jure licitum iri huic Collegio capere, emere, possidere, tenere et in usufructu habere pro usibus et commodis Collegii terras, tenementa, aut alias hereditates et bona personalia, quorum totus annuus reditus decem millia librarum non excedat, ac, si necesse fuerit, eadem vendere, disponere et alienare: necnon pecuniam fœnorare sub satisdatione heritabili aut mobili, reali aut personali, et pro usibus inceptisque Collegii bona resque tenere: præterea omnes chartas, dispositiones, vadimonia aliaque

*First Fellows named in Charter.*

*Power of College to have Common Seal;*

*to hold Lands, etc.*

documenta aut instrumenta quæ attineant ad res heritabiles aut mobiles, reales aut personales, quæ in Collegii beneficium data sint, vel in nomine ejus incorporato, vel a Fiduciariis pro Collegio, teneri posse: omnesque chartas, dispositiones aut alia documenta aut instrumenta a Collegio concedenda, datum iri sub communi sigillo; atque a tribus ex Fiduciariis et vel a Præside vel a Thesaurense vel a Secretario, quicunque his Collegii muneribus pro tempore perfungantur, iri subscriptum.

2. Omnes res heritabiles et mobiles, reales et personales, ubicunque positæ sint, et omnes feudæ chartas, dispositiones, obligationes, instrumenta sasinæ, codicillos locationis, pacta aliaque documenta et instrumenta, et vernaculo sermone "vouchers" earum rerum, aut ad eas spectantia, quæ jam acquisita fuerint a Collegio, aut capta, aut concessa, aut peracta in commodum dicti Collegii Regii Medicorum Edinensis, aut in commodum cujusvis hominis aut quorumvis hominum ut Fiduciarii aut Fiduciariorum, vel aliter, in usum aut in partem dicti Collegii, sive eadem absolute, sive in securitatem, retenta fuerint: et, in universum, omnes res et bona, omnemque pecuniam debitam, obligationes, jura, commoda, libertates, privilegia, et immunitates dicti Collegii et quæ dicto Collegio possidentur, vel quæ a quolibet homine aut quibuslibet hominibus tenentur pro dicti Collegii beneficio, quo tempore hæ literæ conceduntur, transferenda esse, et eadem revera transferri et dari possidenda Collegio Regio Medicorum Edinensi his literis constituto, tam plene quam si eadem acquisita fuissent ab eo Collegio, aut capta, aut concessa, aut peracta in ejus Collegii commodum post hasce literas concessas, eademque omni tempore futuro esse tenenda, dirigenda, vendenda, alienanda, assignanda, locitanda, liberanda aut alio modo disponenda ab eo Collegio sub nomine incorporato " The

## Appendix.

Royal College of Physicians of Edinburgh;" atque nihil opus futurum esse titulo connectente aut continuante aut separato infeofamento aut alio scripto aut processu præter has præsentes literas.

3. Illos qui exsistunt Socii Collegii Regii Medicorum Edinensis tempore, quo hæ literæ conceduntur, Collegii sic constituti primos Socios futuros esse. *Existing Fellows to be first Fellows of the College.*

4. Sociis licitum iri identidem eligere et in Societatem ejus Collegii Sociorum et Membrorum ascribere illos viros quos habiles idoneosque censeant, eo modo, iis temporibus, sub iis regulis, et eo soluto præmio, sicut leges propriæ Collegii, alio atque alio tempore latæ, jusserint. *Fellows to have power to elect Fellows and Members.*

5. Sociis licitum iri identidem in numerum ejus Collegii Permissorum ascribere illos qui cum studiorum curriculum peregerint, et eas probationes subierint, aut sese aliis regulis conformarint, et ea præmia solverint, sicut propriæ Collegii leges, alio atque alio tempore latæ, jusserint: et illos qui Permissi exsistunt Collegii Regii Medicorum Edinensis tempore, quo hæ literæ conceduntur, Collegii sic constituti fore Pemissos. *Fellows to have power to admit Licentiates.*

6. Si aliquo futuro tempore pateret quemvis Collegii Socium aut Membrum in Societatem Collegii Regii Medicorum Edinensis ascriptum fuisse, aut quemvis Permissum in numerum Collegii Permissorum ascriptum fuisse, ex dolo aut fraude aut mendacio, aut alterutrum quamlibet Collegii legem propriam, quamlibet regulam, aut quodlibet præceptum perfregisse, tunc et in omni hujusmodi exemplo, quum is, sive Socius, sive Membrum, sive Permissus, de ea re certior factus et postea auditus fuisset, eo modo, quo, cunctis rebus consideratis, concilio visum fuerit, sociis iri licitum, dummodo tres partes sociorum ex quatuor in toto conventu ad hanc rem convocato concurrant, eum sive Socium, sive Membrum sive Permissum aut censura reprehendere, aut in *Fellows to have power of suspension or expulsion of Fellows, Members, or Licentiates.*

*Procedure for suspension or expulsion.*

cum suspensionis sententiam dicere, prout ei conventui placuerit; aut cum sive Socium, sive Membrum, sive Permissum e Collegio expellere; et tali suspensionis aut expulsionis sententia decreta, istum, sive Socium, sive Membrum, sive Permissum, non amplius fore Socium, Membrum, aut Permissum Collegii; nec habiturum esse aliquod jus nec aliquod beneficium in Collegii bonis et pecunia, aut omnino, aut per temporis spatium quod in suspensionis sententia edictum sit, et omnia jura et privilegia huic, sive Socio, sive Membro, sive Permisso, concessa, prout res se habeat, ex hujusmodi expulsione finitum iri, aut durante hujusmodi suspensione vacatura esse.

<small>Ordinary Meetings of Fellows.</small>

7. Ordinarios Sociorum conventus ad transigenda Collegii negotia iis temporibus advocandos esse quæ, alio atque alio tempore, legibus propriis præscripta fuerint.

<small>Extraordinary Meetings of Fellows.</small>

8. Extraordinarios Sociorum conventus ad considerandum et judicandum quodvis speciale Collegii negotium advocari posse a Præside aut Concilio iis temporibus, ubi opus esse visum fuerit, et extraordinarium Sociorum conventum a Præside advocandum esse, quoties requisitio talem conventum postulans et ejusdem propositum indicans, et a quinque ex Sociis subscripta illi vel Secretario Collegii tradita fuerit, et de omnibus extraordinariis sociorum conventibus præmonendum esse, eo modo, quo leges propriæ jusserint.

<small>Ordinary Meetings of Fellows and Members.</small>

9. Ordinarios Sociorum et Membrorum conventus ad res considerandas quæ ad universæ professionis Medicinæ commodum, commodumque publicum spectent, advocandos esse, iis temporibus, quæ alio atque alio tempore, a legibus propriis præscripta fuerint.

<small>Extraordinary Meetings of Fellows and Members.</small>

10. Extraordinarios Sociorum et Membrorum conventus advocari posse a Præside aut Concilio iis tem-

poribus, quibus opus esse visum fuerit ; et extraordinarium Sociorum et Membrorum conventum a Præside advocandum esse quoties requisitio talem conventum postulans et ejusdem propositum indicans, et a quinque ex Sociis aut Membris subscripta illi vel Secretario Collegii tradita fuerit ; et de omnibus his extraordinariis Sociorum et Membrorum conventibus præmonendum esse eo modo quo leges propriæ jusserint ; et omnes res quæ ad universæ professionis medicinæ commodum commodumque publicum spectent, in aliquo tali Sociorum et Membrorum extraordinario conventu, quatenus in ea requisitione et præmonitione indicatæ fuerint, considerari posse.

11. Concilium Collegii constituendum esse ex Præside et sex Sociis Edinburgi habitantibus aut intra septem millia passuum a domo, vernaculo sermone, "the General Post Office of Edinburgh," appellata, per proximam viam publicam. *Council of College.*

12. Conventum Sociorum quotannis habendum esse, eo die, et ea hora, sicut, alio atque alio tempore, leges propriæ jusserint, ad Præsidem eligendum, et ad eos, qui in Concilio futuri sint, eligendos. *Meeting for election of President and Council.*

13. Eligendos esse a Concilio Collegii Examinatores, etiamque Thesaurensem, Secretarium, vernaculo sermone "Clerk," omnesque alios administros quibus opus fuerit, quotannis et quoties res postulet, si morte, resignatione aut aliter, vacat officium. *Council to elect Office-Bearers.*

14. Eligendos esse a Concilio, annuentibus Sociis, quatuor Socios qui simul cum Thesaurense Fiduciarii futuri sint Collegii ; et quoties, vel morte vel resignatione, vel aliter, officium vacat, Concilio sufficiendum esse alium Socium in prioris Fiduciarii locum ; et dicti Collegii Fiduciarios, tempore quo hæ literæ conceduntur, futuros esse primos, sub his literis, Fiduciarios. *Trustees.*

*Existing Officers to Continue till the first Meeting.*

15. Socios, qui ex Concilio dicti Collegii sunt, tempore quo conceduntur hæ literæ, in eo munere permansuros esse, et futuros esse, sub his literis, primum Concilium; et illum, qui Præses est, eodem tempore, usque in eo munere mansurum esse, et primum sub his literis Collegii Præsidem futurum esse; et illos qui, eodem tempore Thesaurensis, Secretarius, vernaculo sermone " Clerk," ceterique dicti Collegii administri sunt, quemque suum munus retenturum esse, usque ad primum Sociorum annuum conventum ad membra Concilii eligenda, et ad Præsidem eligendum, post has literas concessas, advocandum.

*Vacancies in the Presidentship or Council may be filled up by Fellows.*

16. Si acciderit ut ulla electio Præsidis, aut membrorum Concilii, aut aliquorum ex his, die statuto non facta fuerit, sive ut aliquis Socius, ad alterutrum officium electus, id non acceperit, illum aut illos, qui tunc hoc munere, aut his muneribus perfunguntur, in eodem aut iisdem permansuros esse, donec alius aut alii in eum locum singuli suffecti fuerint; et Socios qui adfuerint in aliquo ordinario conventu, aut in extraordinario conventu, ut in his literis provisum est, advocando, posse eligere aliquem aut aliquos ex Sociis qui eo munere aut iis muneribus fungantur, aut ea eorum munerum parte, quæ nondum impleta fuerit, aut quæ vacaverit quia munus non acceptum fuisset, ut dictum est, pro ea portione unius anni post annuam electionem quæ nondum finita est.

*Filling of vacancies caused by death or resignation.*

17. Si Præses, aut quivis eorum qui in Concilio sunt, mortuus fuerit, aut a munere abdicaverit, ante annum completum aut ante aliud aliquod temporis spatium completum, pro quo electus fuisset, Socios qui adsint in aliquo ordinario conventu aut aliquo extraordinario conventu, ut in his literis provisum est advocando, aut Præsidem, aut membrum Concilii, prout res se habeat, ex

## Appendix

Sociis posse eligere, vice et loco Præsidis aut membri Concilii, qui mortuus fuerit, aut qui a munere abdicaverit : et Socio aut Sociis ita electo aut electis perfungendum esse eo munere aut iis muneribus, per reliquam partem anni post annuam electionem, aut per aliud aliquod temporis spatium, pro quo Præses aut membrum Concilii qui mortuus fuerit, aut qui a munere abdicaverit, electus fuisset.

18. Omnes res, quæ Collegio possidentur, omniaque Collegii negotia gerenda esse atque administranda Sociis et Concilio, eo modo et sub iis regulis, sicut, alio atque alio tempore, leges propriæ jusserint. *Management of property and affairs of College.*

19. Omnia acta facta a Præside, aut ab aliquo Concilii conventu, aut ab aliquo fungente Præsidis munere, aut munere eorum qui sunt in Concilio, etsi postea patuerit aliquod vitium fuisse aut aliquid solennis usus prætermissum fuisse, sive in ejus Præsidis, sive in membri vel membrorum Concilii, electione aut designatione, dum munere fungebantur ut dictum est, aut eos, aut aliquem ex iis, jura ad id munus exercendum non habuisse, aut munus sive Præsidis, sive membri vel membrorum Concilii, eo tempore, vacavisse, habenda esse æque valida, ac si talis Socius jure electus aut designatus fuisset et satis lege polleret et nullum munus vacaret. *Acts of President or Council not to be invalidated by any informality in their election.*

20. Sociis licitum iri, et Nos his literis concedimus illis potestatem et auctoritatem, alio atque alio tempore, decernendi leges proprias (bye-laws), regulas, et præcepta, quæ medicinæ scientiam promoveant, artemque medendi rite dirigant ; quæ decus, ordinem, observantiam Collegio suadeant ; quæ, quomodo eligendi sint Socii, Membra, Permissi, jubeant ; et quæ conditiones qualificationes, sub quibus horum singuli sunt admittendi, describant et proferant ; quæ, quomodo res, pecunia, et negotia Collegii sint administranda, moneant ; quæ omnium conventuum *Fellows to have power to make Bye-Laws.*

et agendi rationum, sive Collegii, sive Concilii et sociorum, sive sociorum et membrorum, sive administrorum Collegii, omniumque muneribus Collegii fungentium ordinem ac leges confirment ; et quæ tempora his conventibus advocandis instituant ; quæ illorum, ex quibus constat corpus societatis, divisionem in ordines, residentium et non-residentium Sociorum et Membrorum, aut aliter, regant ; et quæ his ordinibus assignent eas qualificationes, potestates, privilegia, immunitates et restrictiones quæ Sociis placuerit, alio atque alio tempore, jubere : porro Sociis licitum iri, alio atque alio tempore, abrogare, variare et mutare hasce leges proprias, regulas, præcepta ; dummodo omnis lex propria, regula aut præceptum posthac decernendum, et omnis abrogatio, variatio, aut mutatio, quæ ad aliquam exsistentem legem propriam, regulam aut præceptum attinet, submissa Sociis approbata fuerit in conventu Sociorum ordinario aut extraordinario sub ea forma atque in eo modo, sicut illi identidem constituerint et jusserint.

21. Leges proprias, regulas, præcepta dicti Collegii Regii Medicorum Edinensis quæ existunt sancita, tempore, quo hæ literæ conceduntur, nisi quatenus his literis contradixerint esse et futura esse leges proprias, regulas, et præcepta Collegii his literis constituti, donec aut omnino, aut ex parte abrogata, variata aut mutata fuerint.

22. Collegium ita constitutum et ejusdem Socios, Membra et Permissos, et retinere posse et retenturos, exercituros, et in usufructu habituros esse omnes potestates, munera, jura, et privilegia quæ Collegium Regium Medicorum Edinense aut Socii, Membra, aut permissi ejusdem, antequam hæ literæ concessæ sunt, retinerent aut retinuissent, exercerent aut exercuissent, in usufructu haberent aut habuissent, ex decreto Actorum Parliamenti

in Nostro regno, de quibus supra in his literis mentio facta est.

23. Sequentia verba et verborum formulas in his literis has significationes habitura esse quæ iis infra assignantur; scilicet, "Collegium" significare "Collegium Regium Medicorum Edinense" his literis constitutum; verba "Concilium, Socii, Membra et Permissi" significare singulatim Concilium, Socios, Membra et Permissos Collegii pro eo tempore de quo agatur; verba "leges propriæ" significare et includere leges proprias, regulas, et præcepta Collegii lata aut ferenda, sicut in his literis provisum est.

*Interpretation Clause.*

Et cum Collegii consensu, his literis acceptis significato, et acti Nostri regni primum supra recitati auctoritate, Nos revera, ACCIPIMUS deditionem Nobis factam a Collegio Regio Medicorum Edinensi Chartæ aut Literarum Patentium a Regio Nostro Antecessore Carolo Secundo concessarum, et his literis easdem REVOCAMUS, ABROGAMUS, VACUASQUE REDDIMUS. Et Nos his literis pro Nobis, pro Nostris heredibus, et pro Nostris successoribus, Collegio CONCEDIMUS hanc Nostram Chartam in omnibus rebus et per omnes res futuram esse validam et in lege efficacem secundum verum propositum et ejusdem significationem tenendam, interpretandam et judicandam sensu gratiosiore et utiliore et ad maximum Collegii commodum, non obstante imperfecta quacunque recitatione, aut defectu aut menda aut errore.

*Old Charters revoked.*

Et Nos his literis pro Nobis, pro Nostris heredibus, et pro Nostris successoribus, SPONDEMUS et CONCEDIMUS Collegio, et cum illo CONVENIMUS, Nos, Nostros heredes, et Nostros successores, aliis temporibus et semper posthac, quoties a Nobis Collegium reverenter petiverit atque rogaverit DATUROS et CONCESSUROS ESSE

Collegio omnes alias et ulteriores potestates privilegia et auctoritates, ut efficacior hæc nostra CONCESSIO reddatur, secundum verum harum literarum propositum et significationem, quantum Nos, Nostri heredes, et Nostri successores QUEAMUS et POSSIMUS et quatenus ex rei ratione Jurisconsulti docti legibus Collegii moneant et suadeant.

*This Charter to pass the Seal.*

IN CUJUS REI TESTIMONIUM HUIC PRÆSENTI CHARTÆ NOSTRÆ SIGILLUM NOSTRUM PER UNIONIS TRACTATUM CUSTODIENDUM ET IN SCOTIA VICE ET LOCO MAGNI SIGILLI EJUSDEM UTEND. ORDINAT. APPENDI MANDAVIMUS APUD AULAM NOSTRAM APUD ST JAMES DECINO SEXTO DIE MENSIS AUGUSTI ANNO DOMINI MILLESIMO OCTINGENTESIMO SEXAGESIMO PRIMO ET NOSTRI REGNI VIGESIMO QUINTO ANNI.

Per signaturam manu,
S. D. N. Reginæ suprascriptam.

*Sealed at Edinburgh, the thirty-first day of October, in the year one thousand eight hundred and sixty-one.*

Written to the Seal, and Registered the thirty-first day of October 1861.

JAS. HAY MACKENZIE,
*Depute Keeper of the Seal,*
£80 Scots.

JAMES P. HALLEY,
Depute Director of Chancery.

CRAWFORD AND M'CABE, PRINTERS, EDINBURGH.

www.ingramcontent.com/pod-product-compliance
Lightning Source LLC
Chambersburg PA
CBHW020241170426
43202CB00008B/183